ARE YOU READY?

- Shop the world and buy products tailored to your exact specifications.
- Play tennis with someone a thousand miles away.
- Put yourself into the action at sports events through Virtual Reality.
- Travel anywhere in the world without leaving home.
- Enter into business ventures of cooperation instead of competition, doubling benefits and cutting costs.
- Read newspapers from every city in the world—without the paper.
- Travel the Information Highway to new horizons of ideas, information, and opportunity.

MILLENNIUM APPROACHES

Dennis E. Hensley, Ph.D.

AVON BOOKS
A division of
The Hearst Corporation
1350 Avenue of the Americas
New York, New York 10019

Copyright © 1998 by Dennis Hensley
Published by arrangement with the author
Visit our website at **http://www.AvonBooks.com**
Library of Congress Catalog Card Number: 97-93790
ISBN: 0-380-78703-2

First Avon Books Printing: January 1998

AVON TRADEMARK REG. U.S. PAT. OFF. AND IN OTHER COUNTRIES, MARCA REGISTRADA, HECHO EN U.S.A.

Printed in the U.S.A.

WCD 10 9 8 7 6 5 4 3 2 1

Contents

MILLENNIUM APPROACHES

1: The Momentum of History

A SNOWBALL sent rolling down the side of a mountain will add new snow to itself as it pitches and tumbles its way downward. It eventually will become so huge and so heavy and will gain such speed, it will knock down anything in its path, be it pine tree, animal, sport skier or even log cabin.

History is like that snowball. It, too, gains weight and momentum. People, by necessity, must try to stay ahead of this juggernaut. To do so, people often change their behavior patterns, their value systems, sometimes even their views on life. Back 160 years ago, folks were content to wait five days for a stage-coach to arrive; today, they get upset if they miss one section of a revolving door going into a bank. The pressure of staying "up to speed" is felt every-where.

George Santayana wrote, "Those who ignore history are doomed to repeat it." Cult leader Jim Jones had those words carved in wood and mounted above the large entrance to his compound in Guyana. Iron-ically, Jones and all of his followers died in one day, not because they ignored history, but rather because they didn't pay enough attention to the present and the future.

Therein lies the key to success and survival in the next millennium: One must have an understanding of history, but one's eyes must always be focused on the future. It's a new ball game, with new rules . . . and new penalties.

That is what this book is all about. By putting aside the crystal balls, Ouija boards, astrological charts and New Year's predictions of self-proclaimed seers and mystics, this book examines where society stands today, how it got here, and where the momentum of history is most likely to take it next. This is research, not guesswork. It is factual data, not random speculation. Distilled herein is the wisdom of many of the leading thinkers of eras past and present.

Whatever your current age, you are anticipating being around for the arrival of the new millennium. You wouldn't be reading this book otherwise. And while it can be exciting to look forward to the dawn of a new era, it also can be stressful.

There are equal elements of amazement and fear associated with an understanding of history's momentum. If you doubt that, consider this: The average person lives about seventy-two years. The Wright Brothers made their first successful motorized flight on December 17, 1903. Neil Armstrong set foot on the moon on July 20, 1969. In barely more than sixty-five years—seven years less than one person's lifetime—man advanced from a 120-foot flight to a round trip to the moon. (Today, there are cargo planes that have a wingspan longer than the entire distance of the Wright Brothers' first flight!)

Seeing such rapid advances, we cannot help but wonder what phenomenal things will occur within our own lifetime . . . our children's lifetimes . . . our grandchildren's lifetimes. Will time's momentum become like a snake swallowing its own tail, eventually reaching a point of diminishing return, or will it be possible for there *always* to be something new to discover, to pursue, to improve upon?

Great questions. Well worth pondering. And, fortunately, many people have been doing that for some time now. You'll hear from many of them as you proceed through these chapters.

But before we put the microscope on our current day, let's pause briefly to see what life was like for people of one thousand and two thousand years ago when these great millennial turnovers previously occurred. How futuristic were people back then, and what can we learn from them? And, most important of all, what sort of changes in society have occurred during the two thousand years we are now completing that may serve as road signs to where we are going?

MILLENNIUM APPROACHES ...
FOR B.C. AND A.D.

Had Frank Sinatra been working as a roving minstrel back in the late 990s, it is doubtful he would have been singing "It Was a Very Good Year." For a fact, the period of A.D. 500–1000 has been labeled "The Dark Ages," and with good reason. The Roman Empire had fallen, the general population knew little of classical literature or culture, and the only evidence of organized education was in the monasteries in England, Ireland, France, and Italy. True, Charlemagne did unite Europe, but only for fourteen of these five hundred years (800–814). Times were bad.

If we stay with our symbol of the "snowball" of history, we can see that during the one thousand years prior to that new millennium—those years known as the period "Before Christ" or B.C.—advances were certainly not of "avalanche" proportions. What notable progress there *had* been was primarily limited to the Greeks. Nevertheless, specific breakthroughs in any one field, be it in science or arts or global exploration, often had the effect of moving history along those paths correspondingly.

For example, the perfection of the use of iron for

both tools and weapons around 1130 B.C. led to better shipbuilding and stronger armaments, which, in turn, led the Greeks to exploring, conquering, and settling the entire Ionian coast of Asia Minor. Still, it wasn't until three and a half centuries later that the Greeks moved far enough west to begin establishing settlements in Italy.

The first Olympic games were held in 776 B.C. The structure of patterned music was developed in Greece (reflecting Asian influences) around 750 B.C. Homer composed his epic poems *Iliad* and *Odyssey* shortly thereafter. Around 705 B.C., Greek architects began to construct buildings out of hewn and patterned stone, but it would be another century before artists would begin to form free standing sculptures.

The Greeks created a republic with officials elected for one-year terms in 683 B.C. in Athens; nevertheless, it wasn't until two centuries later (478–477 B.C.) that the Greeks conceived the idea of uniting their various city-states into one formidable nation.

In 534 B.C., the Greek dramatist Thespis (from whom we have derived the word *thespian*, referring to actors) became the father of Greek tragedy by presenting public plays. Actually, they were more like dramatic recitals by a solo figure who recited long passages of narration. It wasn't until 468 B.C. that Sophocles revolutionized stage drama by creating the *cast* (three or more actors performing in a single production).

The concept of philosophy was initiated in 580 B.C. by Thales, but by 399 B.C. the population in Greece demanded the death of its most profound philosopher, Socrates (requiring that he drink hemlock as punishment for poisoning the minds of youths). Socrates was succeeded by his student Plato, who began teaching around 385 B.C. in Athens. Plato's student, in turn, was Aristotle, who served as tutor to Alexander the Great beginning in 343 B.C. and who created his own school for the study of both philosophy and science in 335 B.C.

Political and military shifts resulted in continuous fluctuations of power. By 459 B.C., a rivalry between the city-states of Athens and Sparta had reached full bloom. However, with a military setback for the Athenians at Coronea, it was decided to ask for thirty years of peace between Athens and Sparta, beginning in 445 B.C. This "peace" lasted only until 431 B.C., when full war (known as the Peloponnesian War) broke out between the two states.

A temporary armistice was called for in the year 423 B.C., but fighting resumed the next year. After heavy losses, the Athenians sued for peace in 421 B.C. Ironically, two years later the Athenians again declared war on Sparta. After fifteen more years of combat, both on land and at sea, the Spartans finally defeated the Athenians in 404 B.C.

From 404 B.C. through 371 B.C., the Spartans continued to do battle with other Greek states and neighboring nations. In 382 B.C., the Spartans had successfully gained a foothold in Thebes but were driven out two years later. As a result, Sparta formed an alliance with Thebes in 378 B.C., only to be double-crossed and defeated by that ally in 371 B.C.

In 359 B.C., Philip II ascended to the throne in Macedonia and led his army in quest of regional domination. In 351 B.C., the Athenians resisted Philip, but they were eventually conquered by him in 338 B.C. Two years later, Philip was assassinated and was followed into leadership by his son, Alexander. From 336 B.C. until his death in 323 B.C., Alexander the Great and his armies conquered virtually all of the known civilized world, ranging from the Persian Empire across all of Greece and deep into the Asian continent. At Alexander's death, his generals divided the regions into four sections and reduced the great empire into private provinces of conquest.

What we see, then, in this brief overview, is that change was slow in coming. Even radical change, such as that brought about by war, took decades to accomplish because of the slowness of communication and transportation. Additionally, the shorter life span of individuals, poor sanitation and lack of medications, shallow understanding of science, and nonexistence of compulsory education for the masses, all served to make advancement something that was earned in gradual stages. Yes, the snowball of history was moving forward, but with such slow turnings, its momentum was predictable and very modest by today's standards.

Even into the new millennium, as noted before, humankind did not make startling advances for several centuries yet. Still, the sporadic advances showed evidence of great things to come.

In the year A.D. 105, a discovery was made that would eventually make it possible for you, the reader, to be holding this book as you now are. Paper made from rag fibers was developed by a court servant in China. Its texture, durability, and smoothness allowed for much clearer writing (and painting) to be done on it than on the parchment (or ancient papyrus) being used in Europe and the Middle East at the time. In fact, what made this development so advanced was the fact that paper mills would not come into existence in Europe until the middle 1100s, more than a thousand years later!

The Chinese also figured out in A.D. 190 that pi (the number used universally to determine the circumference of a circle) was 3.14159. Prior to this, mathematicians had estimated it to be approximately 3½. The more accurate figure made everything from architecture to mapmaking much more precise.

During A.D. 100–300, nomadic tribes came from Asia to Europe for raiding, not trading. Both the Roman Empire and the Han Dynasty suffered under the assaults of these invaders. By A.D. 312, the Roman Empire had been divided by Emperor Diocletian into eastern (Italy) and western (Turkey) divisions for the sake of better on-site control. It was that year that Constantine claimed to have had a vision before a great battle that put the words *in hoc signo vinces* ("this sign shows you will be the victor") before his eyes. Thinking the message to have come from God, Constantine credited his subsequent victory to the divine plan of the Creator. As a result, in A.D. 313 he issued the Edict of Milan, giving legal rights and citizen powers to all Christians.

Subsequently, in A.D. 330, Constantine (by then known as "the Great") founded the city of Constantinople on the site of the ancient city of Byzantium (currently known as Istanbul). He served as the Roman Emperor of this division of the empire. It was not until A.D. 395 that the western and eastern divisions of the Roman Empire formally severed all alliances.

In A.D. 408, the Roman army was employing many foreigners as mercenaries. The political leaders feared that since these men were marrying and beginning to have large families, they might one day become greater in number than the Romans themselves. So, to curb this trend, the Romans had the wives and children of these mercenaries executed. Such an act of barbarism only served to turn the mercenaries against the Romans. By the hundreds, they deserted and joined forces with the Visigoth king, Alaric I, who was waging war against the Romans. Two years later, the Visigoths conquered Rome and ransacked it of its wealth and slaves.

The official demise of the Roman Empire came about in A.D. 476, after numerous years of trying to stem the invasions of barbaric tribes from the East. The period following the fall of Rome is often labeled "the Dark Ages" because so much of what had been gained was lost, destroyed, or ignored. Whereas the Romans had developed coined money and a system of universal currency, the barbarians reverted to common barter. The excellent highways laid out by the Romans were now allowed to deteriorate, become overgrown with weeds, and be washed away by storms and wind. The schools and libraries built by the Romans were burned or looted by the barbarians, and the study of art was no longer promoted. Even the established use of Latin as a universal language was lost to the various tribal dialects and foreign tongues being spoken by the conquerors.

The fear put into the peoples of Europe by the invading Vandals, Huns, and Visigoths caused them to develop communities designed for self-preservation. This system was known as feudalism. A lord would select key men to train as knights of his realm. These men would become experts at horseback riding, sword fighting, and jousting. They would serve as the protectors of the farmers, tanners, coopers, wine makers, and other serfs who lived on the lord's estate. At times, the knights from one castle would join forces with the knights of another castle as a means of defeating a common foe. Most often, the serfs of one region stayed their entire lives within the confines of their Lord's property.

In A.D. 507, King Clovis I, leader of the Franks, engaged in battle against Alaric II, king of the Visigoths based in Spain. Alaric II was slain and his army was defeated, allowing Clovis I to claim Gaul (modern France) as his domain. This victory was instrumental in allowing the feudalistic system to continue for centuries thereafter.

On December 25 of A.D. 800, Charlemagne, then king of the Franks, was crowned by the Pope as Emperor of the Romans. Since Charlemagne was of the Christian faith and was a leader of the Roman people, yet was of Germanic heritage, he served to unite the three largest factions of people in Europe during this era. Under this universal bond of kinship, tranquillity was enjoyed for nearly two centuries.

In A.D. 886, a collection of Oriental drawings and Buddhist prayers was collected in book form in China. In A.D. 900, musical harmonics (polyphony) were developed in Europe, replacing the standard one-melody chants with the newer multi-voiced, diversely ranged songs.

Toward the end of that millennium, it was discovered that a "new world" lay beyond Europe to the west. In A.D. 981, the Norwegian sailor and warrior Eric the Red sailed west of Iceland and discovered Greenland. Approximately three years later, his son, Leif Ericson, sailed farther west and landed on the shores of Newfoundland. For the next five centuries, the Norsemen traded with the natives of North America, long before Christopher Columbus would "discover" the East Indies.

The Danish Vikings, under the leadership of Canute II, conquered England in 1013 and ruled it until Canute's death in 1035. The Danes then lost control of England forever.

The famed Crusades were initiated in 1095 by Pope Urban II, when he called upon Christians to travel to the Middle East to drive the followers of Islam out of the Holy Lands and to reclaim Jerusalem and surrounding territories for the followers of Christ. He even promised that anyone dying in battle for this cause would be immediately absolved of all his sins.

The Crusades lasted from 1095 to 1291, costing many lives and never reaching their goal to drive the followers of Islam from the Holy Lands. During the ten-year reign of Richard the Lion-Hearted, however, an agreement was reached that would allow Christians to have visitation and trading rights in the Holy Lands.

If the Crusades proved to be life threatening, they were nothing in comparison to the great killer of the century of the 1300s. Bubonic plague ("the Black Death") ebbed and flowed throughout England, Europe, the Baltic regions, Russia, northern Africa, and the Near East. Estimates ranging from 15 million to 30 million dead have been made. At least 35 percent of the entire population of Europe fell victim to this incurable disease. It was finally discovered that rats and fleas carried the virus and that the mucus formed in the lungs of a victim of the disease could be coughed into the air and transferred to a new victim.

Thus, sick people were required to carry handkerchiefs to cough into and were isolated from noncarriers. Ships coming into ports had to be inspected for rats before docking.

With the eventual ebbing of the plague (it still exists, having evidenced itself in an outbreak in South America as recently as 1992), the residents of Europe turned back to war at the start of the fifteenth century. King Henry V of England defeated the Franks at Agincourt in 1415 and gave England control of most of France thereafter.

Fortunately, war was not the only thing to draw man's attention. From 1350 to 1600, a period we now refer to as "the Age of the Renaissance," the artistic imaginations and scientific explorations of men were on the rise again. Leonardo da Vinci, one of the greatest humans who ever lived (1452–1519), flourished during this time. His paintings (*Mona Lisa* and *The Last Supper*), his inventions (the telescope, the tank), his scientific studies (the flight of birds, the muscle system of humans), and his numerous contributions to art, engineering, and music are highly respected to this very day.

In Mainz, Germany, in 1455, Johannes Gutenberg printed a Bible by using moveable metal type. The ability to reuse the same metal letters made it possible for books to be printed in such quantities that even the common people could own them.

Religion and science took two quantum strides forward during the next century. In 1509, when King Henry VIII could not convince the Pope to grant him a divorce, the king created the Church of England (giving birth to the Protestant movement) and granted his own divorce. In 1543, a Polish astronomer and physicist, Nicolaus Copernicus, wrote a book titled *On the Revolution of the Celestial Spheres* in which he proved mathematically that the earth was not the center of the solar system (as had been believed by all cultures for thousands of years), but rather the sun was.

The following century saw the colonization of the New World. The British established colonies in North America beginning in 1607. The Puritans established their colony at Plymouth, Massachusetts, in 1620. Later that century, back in England, a Bill of Rights was passed in 1689 that guaranteed free elections, open debates in Parliament, trial by a jury of one's peers, opportunities for freedom under reasonable bail fees, and the doing-away-with of cruel and unusual punishments for criminals.

The year 1685 was the birth year of two of the world's greatest composers: George F. Handel, whose *Messiah* was first performed in Dublin, Ireland, in 1742, and Johann Sebastian Bach, whose compositions for keyboard were considered masterpieces both in his lifetime and forever thereafter.

By the eighteenth century, the snowball of progress was beginning to roll forward with ever-increasing velocity. In 1769, James Watt created a steam engine that, in succeeding years, would be enhanced to enable it to pump water out of mines, run heavy machinery in factories, power paddle-wheel boats traversing the rivers, and even run huge locomotives. By 1830, a railroad line was opened between Manchester and Liverpool, England, making use of this steam power. That same year, railroad companies were established in Europe and North America. By 1833, the famed Orient Express was providing rail service from Istanbul to Paris.

The United States had declared its independence in 1776 and earned it after years of battling the British. Less than a century later, however, thirteen of its own states had formed a confederacy and had declared their independence. The United States was eventually reunited, but it took a long war (1860–1865) before the issue was settled. In the process, the slaves in the South were granted their freedom. President Abraham Lincoln was assassinated after the war. Years of reconstruction became necessary before the nation was finally able to recover.

Similar cries of discord were being heard elsewhere during that century. In 1848, Karl Marx and Friedrich Engels wrote their *Communist Manifesto,* calling for the "abolition of private property." This short but powerful book would later provide the philosophical foundation for the communist revolution in Russia.

Science and industry continued to make advances. In 1854, while serving as a nurse during the Crimean War, Florence Nightingale proved that serving wounded soldiers a series of nutritional meals, changing their bed linen every day, sterilizing their bandages, and giving them sponge baths would lead to faster recoveries. Prior to her work, battlefield wounds led to death in nearly one out of every two patients; after her procedures were enacted, fewer than one in twenty battle wounds led to a soldier's death.

In Germany in 1885, a handyman named Karl Benz created a gasoline-powered, three-wheeled vehicle. By 1908 in America, Henry Ford had developed an assembly line procedure that allowed his company to produce Model T automobiles at the rate of one car every seven minutes.

Women's rights became a key issue in many countries. Women were given the right to vote in New Zealand in 1893, but not in America until 1919.

The dropping of a nuclear bomb on Hiroshima in 1945 ushered the world into the Atomic Age. In 1946, the first computer was put into operation at the University of Pennsylvania, using 18,000 vacuum tubes to make it run. A year later, the transistor was invented and the tubes were no longer needed. By the 1960s, personal computers were actively being marketed by several companies. On July 20, 1969, Neil Armstrong set foot on the moon. The computer he used to operate his moon vehicle was less sophisticated than the computers later used for playing video games by children of the 1980s.

And so it continued. . . .

No longer were modest changes being made. History had begun to steamroll itself toward the future. Today, only those who learn to spot the developing trends, ride the waves of change, and understand the ever-developing opportunities for advancement seem to succeed and thrive.

And you can become one of those people. As noted previously, this book provides you with a blueprint for future success. If you've felt "out of the loop" regarding futurism, you can now be brought up to speed.

We will begin in an entertaining way by looking at what the novelists during past eras predicted the world of the future would be like. Many, amazingly, were right on target, whereas others were so far off the mark, it was outright laughable.

Next, we will see which religious movements are gaining a foothold as we approach the new millennium. We will find out what questions people are asking about faith, religion, worship, and humankind's relationship with a higher power. In many ways, the anxiety over the coming of a new millennium is having a direct impact on people's yearning for a relationship with a power beyond themselves.

Next, we will look at the six most powerful forces of economic change that are now evolving and that, consequently, will have the greatest impact on your wallet. You will see how you can protect your earnings, provide more efficiently for your family, and also understand why the coming generations will have a lot to worry about financially.

In other chapters, we will examine the art, music, literature, and sports of the next millennium. If you are curious as to how you will "have fun" after the year 2000, you will find your answers in these chapters.

By necessity, we will spend considerable time examining the technology of the present and future. In many ways, technological advances have provided the best medical treatment, home security, and auto safety we have ever known. However, many of those same advances have led to job eliminations, the de-humanizing of work environments, and a hypnotic control of our young people. Whether technology ultimately proves to be your friend or foe will often depend on how much you know about it.

The examination of how families and communities and nations are changing, both positively and negatively, will be studied as we near the end of the book. Additionally, you will be shown specific things you can do, individually, to prepare yourself for the vastly different kind of life that awaits you in the next millennium.

Some things in this book will surprise you. Other things will cause you to pause and think about your relationship with the world around you. Yet other things will entertain you and make you eager to discover everything you can about living in the twenty-first century.

Years ago, a poem was written about six blind men who each touched an elephant on a different part of its body. One man, who felt the thick leg, declared that the elephant was like a mighty tree trunk; a second man, who felt the elephant's tail, declared the elephant to be like a woven rope. A third man, who felt the elephant's tusks, declared the elephant to be like a log. And so it continued, with each man being accurate about only that section of the elephant he had had contact with. No man truly had the big picture of what the elephant really looked like.

Many people are approaching the future this same way. If they study the future at all, they study it solely from the perspective of the specific areas they are personally interested in. This results, however, in tunnel vision. This book will reveal the whole picture to you—from events in your neighborhood to what is occurring on the opposite side of the globe. You'll be told the way things began, how they developed, and where they are going.

It is guaranteed to be a fascinating trip.

Turn the page.

Ride that snowball.

2: How the Literary Dreamers Predicted the Future

"THE REASON I think so much about the future," wrote engineering genius Charles F. Kettering, "is because I expect to spend the rest of my life there."

Like Kettering, many men and women have given serious thought over the ages to what the future would be like—yea, even what it *should* be like. In some instances, these imaginative futurists were amazingly accurate in their predictions, even though scoffed at by their contemporaries.

Circa 1920, for example, Franz Kafka wrote a novel called *The Trial* in which a man named Joseph K. was arrested. He continually asked to be told what his crime was, but was given no answer other than the fact that he was worthy of judgment. He was subsequently put on trial (for what?) and found guilty (of what?). He was taken to a stone quarry for execution, where he was stabbed in the heart. He died never knowing what his crime was, other than being who he was.

Readers thought this was an absurd novel, absolutely ridiculous. They saw no logic to it or any viable correlation to real life. Then only two decades later in Germany, the Nazis began to arrest Jews, Gypsies, and the mentally disabled and to herd them into concentration camps for execution. When the prisoners asked what their "crime" was, they were told it was the crime of being who they were. Suddenly, Kafka had become a prophet.

In a much earlier example, Jules Verne at age 35 wrote a novel in 1863 called *Paris in the 20th Century*. In his futuristic setting of 1963, Verne predicted that Paris would have gas-powered automobiles, an elevated monorail, fax machines, airplanes, televisions, and computers. He predicted that prisons would execute prisoners with an electric chair (this being written twenty-five years before the first electric chair was used in the U.S. for an execution).

When Verne's manuscript was submitted to his publisher, Jules Hetzel, it was rejected because the company's editors thought it was too preposterous. They called it bleak, soulless, and very much far-fetched. Verne locked it away and went on to write *From the Earth to the Moon*, in which he predicted that the first successful launch of a rocket to the moon would be from Florida, and *Twenty Thousand Leagues under the Sea*, in which he predicted the development of submarines capable of carrying hundreds of men and going miles below the ocean's surface. (Finally, in 1994, Verne's rejected manuscript about Paris was rediscovered and published by Hachette Livre.)

Kafka and Verne and others of their ilk carried the biblical adage one step further: "A prophet is not without honor, save in his own land . . . and in his own era."

Knowing how insightful writers of previous ages have been in predicting the future, or how entertaining they have been about it even when they have been wrong, it is worth spending a little time reexamining utopian writings and works of futurism. Naturally, we cannot in this limited space touch on all such works, but a look at respective samples will give us the flavor of such writings.

Sir Thomas More coined the word "utopia," meaning both "no place" and/or "a place where everything is fine" when he wrote *Utopia* in 1516. It was published in Latin in Paris, Basle, Vienna, Venice, and

Florence but not translated into English until 1551 (some sixteen years after More had been executed for not assisting with a divorce action for the King of England).

More's *Utopia* is separated into Books I and II. The first book points out the evils in England during More's day, including the decline of agriculture and the rise of industry, the conversion to sheepherding from farming, and the problems of massive unemployment and wide-scale poverty. The second book offers solutions to all these problems.

On the island of Utopia, the workday is only six hours long so that people can have time for art, reading, and conversation; slavery is outlawed except for people caught in adultery or enemy soldiers captured on the field of battle; war is avoided if at all possible; all religious beliefs are tolerated; the king is elected (for life) by the people, and he always rules in a way that benefits the majority of citizens; parents are encouraged to punish wayward children, and husbands are allowed to discipline wives in whatever way is necessary to keep them in line; and all citizens, including the king, must do some sort of productive work each day that will be of benefit to the state and its people.

Many of the concepts found in More's *Utopia* are not original but are adapted from and expanded upon what is found in Plato's *The Republic*, written in approximately 370 B.C. Plato's republic established reason (rational thinking, logic) as the only basis for discerning truth and, thus, providing a way of deciding what was right and what was wrong and how to solve human problems. This applied to art, ethics, politics, social issues, psychology, finances, and even science.

Plato argued that a moral life guaranteed happiness. He admitted that it was hard to be moral and just if one's government was evil and corrupt. As such, he proposed that a republic should be created wherein justice was truly practiced. It should begin, he felt, with city-states that had each person doing just one job, but doing it perfectly. Thus, the worker would enjoy his career, and the state would receive excellent service and goods. Citizens would be separated into three specific categories: artisans (craftsmen and laborers), auxiliaries (military soldiers and sailors), and rulers (government leaders). Everyone— men *and women*—would be given a public education and would rise through the ranks of commerce or politics according to his or her academic capabilities.

Women were not to be given complete liberation, however. Marriage would be outlawed, and men could have free access to all women. All women getting pregnant would give up their children to the care of and rearing by the state. The country would be led by a ruler who was a philosopher, for only a philosopher would be able to see both sides of an issue fairly and, thus, be able to make appropriate judgments.

Though Plato's *The Republic* and More's *Utopia* were far from practical concepts, they stimulated additional thinking along the lines of how utopian societies might be developed. Subsequent works included *The City of the Sun* (1623) by Tommaso Campanella, *The New Atlantis* (1627) by Francis Bacon and *Social Contract* (1762) by Jean-Jacques Rousseau.

Since then, each age and era has produced its own array of utopian parodies (Jonathan Swift's *Gulliver's Travels*, Lewis Carroll's *Alice's Adventures in Wonderland*) or utopian experimental communities (Samuel Butler's *Erewhon*, Nathaniel Hawthorne's *The Blithedale Romance*) or utopian tales of technological marvels (Arthur C. Clarke's *2001: A Space Odyssey*, Robert A. Heinlein's *Starship Troopers*) or utopian horror stories (Ray Bradbury's *Fahrenheit 451*, Anthony Burgess's *A Clockwork Orange*).

Since our current focus is on life in the coming millennium, we can get the best "feel" for what the literary dreamers of 1885–1950 were imagining if we examine five novels that drew immediate widespread attention in their own day and are still continuing to attract vast reading audiences today: *Looking Backward* by Edward Bellamy, *The Time Machine* by H. G. Wells, *The Iron Heel* by Jack London, *Brave New World* by Aldous Huxley, and *1984* by George Orwell.

LOOKING BACKWARD BY EDWARD BELLAMY (1888)

Though not read as much today as it was fifty to eighty-five years ago, no utopian book has had more of an immediate impact on society as has *Looking Backward*. After its publication, more than 150 "Bellamy Clubs" were formed in the U.S. to discuss ways of implementing the philosophies and concepts developed by Edward Bellamy. So popular was he, Bellamy traveled nationwide delivering lectures at these clubs and at schools and libraries for nearly three years non-stop. Already in frail health, the grueling schedule proved to be exhaustingly fatal, causing his premature death at age forty-eight. Interestingly, because he was so wealthy from the royalties on the literally millions of copies of his book that were selling, and because he so wholeheartedly believed in his cause, Bellamy never charged an honorarium for his speeches.

Looking Backward tells the story of a foppish Boston aristocrat named Julian West who has inherited a fortune from his grandfather's stock investments. West does no work nor feels any compulsion to do anything except read, correspond with friends, and go on outings or attend dinner dates with his fiancée, Miss Edith Bartlett. Edith, too, is from a very wealthy family and, thus, expects to live in high style once she and Julian are married. To that end, Julian hires an architect and a contractor and designs a magnificent mansion for Edith and him to reside in after their marriage. Work begins immediately; but, to Julian's great frustration, a series of labor strikes continually slows down the progress of the structure.

Julian suggests that he and Edith simply advance the date of their wedding, get married, and then go away to Europe and other exotic locales on an extended honeymoon until their dream house has been completed. Julian's disdain for the striking laborers is never disguised.

On Decoration Day in 1887, Julian accompanies Edith and her family to the grave site of Edith's older brother, a casualty of the Civil War. After leaving a wreath, they go back to the Bartlett home and have dinner. Edith sees that Julian has not slept well for several nights, he being an insomniac, so she sends him home at 9 P.M. with orders that he go right to bed.

Once home, Julian sends his black manservant, Sawyer, out to retrieve a hypnotist named "Doctor" Pillsbury. Julian dresses for bed and retreats into a special bunker he has built below the foundation of his house. The bunker has thick cement walls and a cement foundation under the floor. The roof is made of stone slabs hermetically sealed. The door is of solid iron coated with asbestos. A ventilation pipe with a miniature circulation windmill runs out the top.

The bunker serves two purposes: first, it acts as a vault for Julian West's personal papers and valuables; second, it blocks out all the sounds of the outside world that might prevent Julian from getting a good night's sleep. Despite this solitude and quietude, Julian still needs the assistance of a hypnotist to put him into a trance in order to get undisturbed rest. Sawyer is given instructions to wake Julian at 9 A.M., and then Pillsbury puts Julian into a very deep trance.

Once he is in the trance, Julian's bodily functions reduce themselves to near-zero activity. His heart seldom beats, he breathes only occasionally, and he never moves.

That night, Julian's home burns to the ground. No one left alive knows of the existence of the bunker. The destroyed home is dismantled, the ground is sold, and a new structure is built at that location. Finally, Julian wakes up one day to discover that he is no longer in the bunker. He is in the home of a Dr. Leete, who informs Julian that he has been in a trance for 113 years, 3 months and 11 days. It is now September 30, 2000. The bunker was discovered when Dr. Leete hired crewmen to excavate his backyard so that he could create a duck pond. Once opened, the bunker was found to contain Julian West, whom Dr. Leete revived.

Julian is astounded at the way Boston has changed—tall, modern buildings; wide thoroughfares—but he is even more astounded by the ways society has changed. He discovers that men and women are now equals in voting, owning land, and attending school. He discovers that nationalism has replaced capitalism and that all people, no matter what their occupation, make exactly the same amount of annual income. Retirement begins at age forty-five, except for certain crucial professions. The government owns all factories and businesses and employs legions of bureaucrats to manage the daily affairs of running the country.

People's attitudes and behavior are also radically changed. People do not lie or cheat. They are concerned with culture and learning and refinement, not with the accumulation of material goods, as they were in Julian's era. The women dress in comfortable clothes; no longer are they laced tightly into bodices and surrounded by hooped skirts and made to wear elaborate feathered hats and lace veils. Men are not separated into working-class people and upper-class wealthy nonworkers.

Though it takes him some time to adjust, Julian finally comes to see that the new developments have forged a society far superior to the one he had known.

He is content to be living in A.D. 2000. He finds new friends and a new love and new personal meaning to his life.

Whereas Bellamy did not term his work a proposal for communism or socialism, it was instrumental in causing the temporary success of the Populist Party at the polls. His novel insisted that mankind could evolve into a more sharing and open society, if given enough time and education. This differs, of course, from communist teachings which insist that a revolt from the lower classes is first necessary in order to wrest control of the government from the nobles or the capitalists.

Bellamy's aim was to create a society in which each person would be equal to everyone else and would have the same benefits and opportunities, yet each would still be independent enough to develop his or her personal talents for the betterment of all. In theory, this sounds very worthwhile. In practice, however, as the fall of the U.S.S.R. has proven, most people do not want to be content; they constantly want to have new goals, new acquisitions, new rewards. Competition, not altruism, seems to be more the innate nature of man.

There is value in reading Bellamy's book today. It warns us to examine our current way of life so as to discern whether or not we have pulled a joke on ourselves. For example, the two-income family has become a way of life today; thus, we are now working twice as hard to obtain the material goods that are supposed to provide us with "the good life." Can this really be "the good life," however, if we are always tired, always working, and always away from those we love? Isn't that enslavement? Certainly Bellamy would say so. It is these sorts of "in your face" issues that Bellamy forces his readers to confront, and that is why his "look backward" continues to help us know how to look forward.

The Time Machine by H. G. Wells (1895)

Interestingly, *The Time Machine* was the first novel written by H. G. [Herbert George] Wells, and, despite being very short, it helped earn Wells the title of "The Father of Science Fiction." The book was written seven years after Wells graduated from college.

Wells was born in Bromley, Kent, England, on September 21, 1866, the son of a lady's maid and an unsuccessful shopkeeper who also played professional cricket. When H. G. was only thirteen, he was pulled from school and made an apprentice to a dry goods merchant. The work was repetitive and tedious, and Wells hated it. His intelligence needed greater challenges, so he applied for a scholarship to the Normal School of Science in London and was accepted. While there, one of his teachers was Thomas Henry Huxley, whose grandson Aldous would later become famous as the author of the futuristic novel *Brave New World*.

Wells graduated with a bachelor's degree in biology in 1888 and became a poorly paid science teacher. He supplemented his income by coauthoring a science textbook and by writing freelance science articles. In his late twenties, Wells was diagnosed with tuberculosis, and he also suffered a kidney injury during a soccer match. His poor health forced him to resign his teaching position. Earlier, in 1891, Wells had written two essays for *Fortnightly Review*. When that periodical's editor, Frank Harris, later became editor of the *Saturday Review of Literature*, he suggested that Wells should write about speculative science—future developments, new machines, medical breakthroughs, and advancing technology.

This greatly appealed to Wells. He began writing short stories, novellas and novels at an astounding pace—one book per year between 1895 and 1946, as well as editorials, essays, reviews, social commentary, political pamphlets, and educational monographs. All tallied, he wrote more than four million words of fiction and more than eight million words of nonfiction.

After his death in 1946 at age eighty, Hollywood discovered the works of H. G. Wells and made full-length motion pictures of *The Invisible Man, Food of the Gods, War of the Worlds, The Island of Dr. Moreau, The First Men in the Moon,* and, naturally, *The Time Machine.*

Although many of Wells's works, such as *Men Like Gods, The Shape of Things to Come,* and *When the Sleeper Awakes,* are futuristic, it is *The Time Machine* that has remained the most popular among readers. For a fact, there isn't much solid science found in *The Time Machine,* for time travel has always been impossible. That, however, was not the focus of Wells's book. The way in which his Time Traveller arrived in the future was not important to Wells; what really mattered was what Wells speculated the Time Traveller would find in the future.

The novel begins at the home of the Time Traveller, a man never given a name but described as someone very knowledgeable of physics, mathematics, and engineering. He is an inventor by avocation and a man who enjoys lively, educated conversation. To that end, he has developed a circle of diverse professional men who meet at his home on Thursdays for dinner and drinks, and lively debate. Except for a red-haired man named Filby, who serves as devil's advocate in many conversations, the guests are identified only by occupational labels—i.e., the Provincial Mayor, the Medical Man, the Psychologist, and a person well-read in classical literature, who is called "the Very Young Man."

At one of these dinner parties, the Time Traveller explains that, in theory, time can be considered a tangible fourth dimension that can be measured like the other three (height, width, length) and, thereby, traversed like the other three. To prove his point, he brings out a small model of a machine that he purports can follow the fourth dimension line and, thus, go into the future or past. He throws a lever and, sure enough, the machine disappears. His friends applaud and congratulate him on his sleight-of-hand trick. He protests that it isn't a trick, but they remind him that he has done this sort of joke before, once even making a "ghost" appear.

To prove his theory, the Time Traveller invites the men back to dinner the next Thursday, at which time he will have been to the future and back. The men wink at each other and chuckle, yet agree to return. This they do, only this time bringing a newspaper editor named Mr. Blank, a reporter and another unnamed witness. Although dinner awaits them, their host is absent. They eat without him.

Near the conclusion of the meal, the Time Traveller staggers into the room. He is bruised and has a facial cut; his hair and clothes are dirty and smeared with something green; his complexion is pale, and he seems half dazed; he walks with a limp. After swallowing two full glasses of wine, he excuses himself to get washed and to put on clean clothes. Shortly, he returns, eats a large dinner, then sits back to tell the story of his trip to the year A.D. 802,701.

The narrator explains that using quartz, ivory, brass, and ebony, he built a large-scale version of the time machine model he had previously shown the men. Mounting it, he pushed the lever forward, and suddenly months and seasons began to zip by him like individual ticks of a second hand. He zoomed so quickly through the centuries, he had to pull hard on the lever to make the machine stop. The sudden stop threw him from the machine.

He found himself in a futuristic world that had taken pampered aristocratic society to its ultimate extreme. These people were now only a yard or so tall, very pale and thin, unthinking and uncaring. They simply idled time away by playing, dancing, singing, and lounging. They lived on the earth's surface and were called the Eloi.

Counterpointing the Eloi were the Morlocks, who were the ultimate extreme in the evolution of common laborers. They were hairy, bulky, muscular, apelike creatures who lived belowground or in caves. They maintained the machines that kept the planet functioning. Also, they were cannibals, and their main supply of food was the population of the Eloi.

The Time Traveller admits he was dumbfounded by all this. On the one hand, he was overjoyed to discover that he was in a time and place in which there were no wars, no poverty, no diseases, no pestilence, and no lack of food. All around him were marvelous structures of glass and chrome, tall towers and buildings of the most sophisticated architectural design.

On the other hand, he was appalled at the way the upper class had become so pathetically weak, both physically and mentally, and at the way the lower class had become animalistic, isolated, and barbaric.

He decided he must leave. To his horror, he discovered that the Morlocks had pulled his time machine inside a huge white sphinx of theirs and had sealed off the entrance by locking two huge brass doors. With bravery and cunning, and using the brightness of fire as his chief weapon, the Time Traveller sneaked inside the sphinx during a roundup of Eloi. Adventures ensued, and eventually the man found his machine and was able to return to his own time. He arrived back home, showing obvious evidence of his fights with the Morlocks.

After telling his story, his companions tell him he should be writing novels, for he sure knows how to spin a very imaginative tale. Realizing that they don't believe him, the Time Traveller shows them a flower he has brought back from the future, unlike anything anyone has ever seen. He then leads them to the work room and shows them the machine. It looks dirty and nicked, but it does not convince them it has been traveling through time. Everyone goes home, not believing a word of the story.

The next day one man come back to the home of the Time Traveller. He finds the Time Traveller loaded down with a camera, film, notebooks and other proof-gathering materials. He insists he is going back across time to prove he can do it. The visiting man sits alone in the dining room for awhile, then goes to find the Time Traveller in his laboratory. As he opens the door, he sees a shimmering image of a fading machine and man. A roar is heard, a skylight is blown out, and the room is suddenly empty.

For the next three years, the friend returns at regular intervals to the laboratory of the Time Traveller, hoping to see his neighbor again. Alas, the inventor never returns. His friend often speculates: Did he go back in time and get killed by a dinosaur; did he go ahead in time and get captured and eaten by the dreaded Morlocks? No one will ever know.

Although *The Time Machine* can be read as a saga of scientific adventures, Wells also was trying to make readers think about the pro and con aspects of the advance of technology when it outdistances the advance of sociology. Are machines created as labor-saving devices meant to replace man's own thinking and working capacities? And should one class of society be given exclusive access to the benefits of these machines while another class exists only to perform maintenance on them?

Such questions were worthy of contemplation in 1895 when *The Time Machine* was first published. They are still worthy of contemplation today. And that's probably why the book has been in print for more than a century. It entertains us *and* makes us think.

THE IRON HEEL BY JACK LONDON (1908)

One of the most interesting, and yet perplexing, futuristic novels to be written at the beginning of the twentieth century was Jack London's *The Iron Heel*. London began work on the book in 1906 and saw it published in 1908. It received poor reviews, and initial sales were modest at best; yet the book has never been out of print and today is available in a wide range of languages. Its literary style is flowery, its main character is shallow, and the book is overly heavy with political speeches. Still, it has vibrancy and boldness that make it appealing to many readers.

The book's plot, theme, and message seem at first to be contradictory to London's own political and social beliefs. From age seventeen until his formal resignation (by letter) from the Socialist Party just before his death at age forty, London wrote and spoke out on behalf of workers' rights and socialistic legislation.

In his high school literary magazine, *The Aegis*, London wrote essays and works of fiction that exposed the plight of working-class people at the hands of the robber-baron capitalists. During most of his life, he signed his letters, "Yours for the Revolution." He lectured at Yale and Harvard and on other campuses in favor of the socialist cause and twice ran for Mayor of Oakland, California (losing both times), as a Socialist.

Despite all this empathy for the lower classes, London owned a vast tract of land in Sonoma Valley, California. He hired an Oriental manservant, and he kept company with famous actresses, poets, publishers, journalists, and other upper-class citizens. He even built himself a huge mansion called "Wolf House," which cost seventy thousand dollars. The house was burned the day before Jack and his second wife, Charmian, were to have moved in, and one of the suspicions that has lingered has been that a brother socialist torched it to try to get London to turn from his capitalist ways.

Even though London predicted in his lectures and writings that the working class would seize power in America by uniting at the ballot box and going to Washington en masse, he slowly came to see that the economically mighty capitalists would never permit this to happen. So it is, then, that London's novel, paradoxically, chronicles the *failed* efforts of a movement to overthrow the capitalist stronghold in America.

The manuscript of *The Iron Heel* is purported to have been discovered seven hundred years after the twentieth century, during an age when socialism finally does rule the world. The book is given a preface and a series of footnotes by an imaginary futuristic historian, but the main body of the text is supposedly written by Mrs. Avis Everhard, wife of the late Ernest Everhard, whom the book is about.

In the story, from 1912 to 1932, a wild-eyed band of socialists, primarily made up of slum dwellers and idealistic revolutionaries, wages a guerilla war against the "Iron Heel," the financially powerful oligarchy made up of the forces of ruthless capitalism, organized religion, and subsidized labor unions. The socialists are led by Ernest Everhard, a brawny and dynamic intellectual.

At first, Everhard tries to gain followers by writing pamphlets and giving speeches. As a dinner guest at a wealthy man's home, Everhard uses wit and his agile tongue to defeat a group of clergymen who try to debate him on metaphysical religious matters. Everhard tells them that if ministers really practiced the teachings of Christ, they would be using the church coffers to feed, clothe, house, and educate the poor. (Later, one minister from this group tries to adhere to this calling but only becomes defrocked and then locked inside an insane asylum.)

Also at this dinner is Avis Cunningham, daughter of a professor of physics at the University of California at Berkeley. Ernest tells her of a laborer who lost an arm working in one of the factories in which the Cunninghams have investments. The worker was fired and given no medical benefits. Avis insists this must be a lie. She subsequently visits the worker and discovers that he is but one of hundreds of workers who have been maimed on the job but who were given no compensation. In her outrage, Avis writes a factual report of these events. To her amazement, no newspapers will print it, fearing the loss of advertising revenue from capitalist-owned factories.

Ernest Everhard lectures before "The Philomaths," an organization of the community's wealthiest businessmen. He denounces their callousness and tells them the voters will rise up and seize control. In response to this, a spokesman for the group tells Everhard flatly that in such a case, these men would hire mercenaries to use shrapnel and machine-gun fire to "grind you revolutionaries down under our heel, and we shall walk on your faces." The man then states emphatically, "The world is ours, we are its lords, and ours it shall remain . . . !"

Fueled by his anger, Everhard now takes his message to the common folk, urging them to join unions, stage strikes, and vote for the Socialist Party. The oligarchy does not consider Everhard a serious threat until after the next national election when fifty-one Socialist Party congressmen, including Everhard himself, are voted into office.

At first, Ernest and Avis, now a couple, are ecstatic over this turn of events; but it doesn't take long for reality to set in. With no power in the White House or the Senate, and only one vote in nine in the House, the Socialist Party is powerless to pass any significant new legislation. Even worse, the oligarchy has now started to make good on its threat to hire mercenaries to physically assault the socialists. Mobs attack socialist newspapers and destroy their presses. Anyone known to be a member of the Socialist Party or to have voted socialist is fired from his job. Anyone making a pro-labor speech in a public place is arrested by bribed police officers, taken to jail, and then secretly murdered.

The workers try to unite, but when they strike a factory, the state militia and U.S. Army are brought in to assist the local police in breaking the strike. Any worker trying to hold the line is shot dead, wounded, or arrested and placed in a concentration camp. Throughout all this, no protests are heard from clergymen, college professors, or newspaper editors.

Meanwhile, as a ploy to draw attention away from domestic problems, the capitalist press and its masters decide to create a war against Germany. The plan is to break the unions by getting workers to serve in the army and, simultaneously, to take away many of the world commerce markets controlled by German manufacturers. The common people in both Germany and America see through this ruse, and neither country is able to raise a large enough army to stage a transatlantic war.

Having failed at the war effort, the oligarchy decides to create a scenario in which the workers will turn against each other. They succeed in this. The large unions in the country are given shorter work weeks, better working conditions, and higher wages, but the smaller unions are given nothing. As a result, all of the small unions lose their members and become defunct. Subsequently, the larger unions are turned against, one at a time, until all are eradicated.

Everhard now sees that the only hope for the common workers is for them to pick up weapons and to counterattack the ruling class. Everhard, himself, forms several commando units and terrorist squads. Although they have a just cause and are dedicated to each other, the socialists have no money, no rifles, no bullets, no cannons, no medical or food supplies, no combat experience. The oligarchy, however, has limitless resources. It raises a massive private army aptly named "the Mercenaries."

The Mercenaries, determined to make a show of force, attack a large socialist commune in Chicago. The men of the commune grab pickaxes, hatchets, kitchen knives, hammers, and sticks of wood, and retaliate. It becomes a bloodbath, with the professional soldiers slaughtering hundreds of the poorly trained, poorly equipped socialists. Thus ends the First Revolt.

Ernest Everhard goes underground and forms a new group of followers. Once trained and ready, they lead the Second Revolt. Everhard, however, is captured and executed by the Mercenaries. His followers are defeated, and Avis sequesters herself in Sonoma Valley, where she writes this biography of her noble husband's life and failed efforts at reform. The manuscript stops in midsentence, unfinished. It is not explained how Everhard was actually captured. The manuscript is said to have been hidden in a hollow log of the cabin where it was discovered seven hundred years after the twentieth century, in the year 419 B.O.M. (Brotherhood of Man).

Much of *The Iron Heel* is pseudo-autobiographical. Ernest Everhard is described as having a blacksmith's biceps, a boxer's neck, and a head of thick blond hair: an exact physical description of Jack London. Everhard's speeches throughout the book espouse London's own discipleship of Karl Marx and Herbert Spencer. Even the love affair between Ernest and Avis is a parallel to Jack's relationship with Charmian, his "mate woman."

At the end of the novel, Ernest Everhard (like Jack London) realizes he and his followers are doomed to lose the Second Revolt. Still, in defiance, Everhard screams, "We have lost a battle, we shall win the war. Lost for this time, but not forever! We have learned many things. Tomorrow the cause will rise once more, stronger in wisdom and in discipline."

Though London gives such a powerful statement to his main character, the fact remains that *The Iron Heel* presents a graphic picture of a failed socialistic effort throughout the entire century. But why would London paint such a picture if he, himself, was such an avid socialist?

The answer lies in the fact that London could not escape his training as a journalist. As a reporter, he covered the Russo-Japanese War, the San Francisco earthquake, the Mexican Revolution, the gold rush to the Yukon, and even the Jeffries-Johnson title bout. He learned how to see things as they were and to report them with clarity and accuracy. The same held true of the socialist movement. As Jack saw the Supreme Court rule against unions, as he saw socialist candidates lose at the polls, as he saw Pinkertons break strikes nationwide, he concluded that it would be a long time (if ever) before a workers' revolt would succeed in America.

In 1903, a man named W. J. Ghent wrote a book called *Our Benevolent Feudalism*. He predicted that as the Industrial Revolution's momentum saw more and more factories come into existence, laborers would be bound to the machines of their employers the same way serfs had been bound to the farmland of their lords. But Ghent saw this as something good, because he felt the factory owners would eventually see the benefit of wanting to maintain a healthy and productive workforce. As such, the capitalists would provide decent pay and adequate benefits for workers.

Jack London read this book and saw the wisdom in it. London agreed that factory workers would become the new serfs, but he disagreed with the notion that the factory owners would be benevolent. London felt that as one group of workers became too old, too tired, or perhaps too injured to be of good service any longer, it would be discarded and replaced by younger and stronger persons who also desperately needed jobs. The rich would stay rich, and the poor would stay poor. Only a violent overthrowing of the whole system would ever change things . . . and *that* would require money, supplies, and trained leaders, all of which were in short supply in the Socialist Party in 1906, when London began to write *The Iron Heel*.

What, then, did Jack London accomplish in writing this book? In truth, not much. As a novel, it is poorly written, lacking the pace, beauty, and raw power of London's earlier works, *The Call of the Wild*, *White Fang*, and *The Sea-Wolf*. As a work of propaganda, it was of no interest to the capitalists, and it was truly depressing to the socialists. And, as a window to the future, it didn't accurately predict any of the socialistic changes that *would* occur in America (Social Security, Medicare, welfare, Aid to Families with Dependent Children, school lunch programs, unemployment compensation). Its only redeeming quality lies in the fact that during these times there *were* many angry, suppressed, non-unionized, poorly paid laborers who lacked the education and talent to explain their plight to the world. Jack London, through his novel, became their spokesman. And laborers everywhere still honor him for that.

BRAVE NEW WORLD BY ALDOUS HUXLEY (1932)

Though he only started out to write a parody of the science-fiction novels of H. G. Wells, Aldous Huxley soon became very serious about the story that started evolving from his pen. In *Brave New World*, Huxley accurately predicted what the eleven most pressing problems of the future would be; furthermore, his prediction of how future generations might choose to cope with these problems were, in many cases, chillingly accurate.

The novel opens six centuries into the future, in the year 632 A.F. (After Henry Ford). Time is marked in honor of Ford for two reasons: first, because Ford was the man who made the assembly line a way of life, something crucial to the existence of Huxley's Utopia; and second, because Ford once stated, "History is bunk," which is a credo of these future-looking citizens of Utopia.

Following a devastating global war that lasted nine years and poisoned the earth with germ warfare, a new way of life was instituted. Ten men now serve as "Controllers" of the world. Under them are five classes of citizens who are developed as test-tube babies. The Alpha and Beta citizens are those created for intellectual ruling; Gamma and Delta citizens are created for middle and lower management functions; and Epsilons are created as muscular morons who do all the manual labor. The world motto is "Community, Identity, Stability."

Although this world society is advanced in many

ways (rocket-ship travel between continents, elimination of disease and aging and war and crime), it knows nothing of nuclear power. Although women are unable to get pregnant, people are encouraged to enjoy sex with whomever they take a fancy to. Marriage has been abolished, and all children are wards of the state [see Plato's *Republic*].

The story begins with a group of children being given a tour by the Director of Hatcheries and Cloning (DHC) of his facilities. He explains how fertilized eggs in test tubes move down a conveyor belt over a 267-day development period (ironically, this equals a nine-month pregnancy), during which they are modified by different injections to create exactly the kind of new citizens needed for specific jobs. When children are born, they are cared for by nurses who make sure that they are fed subconscious messages via taped recordings played during the child's sleep, year after year. Emotions are not tolerated; if children or adults feel overjoyed or upset, they are encouraged to swallow *soma* pills, a drug that is part tranquilizer and part hallucinogen.

Working at the hatchery is a purple-eyed woman named Lenina, who has skin blotches caused by lupus, a common female blood disorder. She is considered very attractive, however, and many of the men, including the DHC, arrange sexual encounters with her. One of her coworkers, Bernard Marx, invites her to go by rocket with him to a wilderness in New Mexico, America. This is the place to which all savages have been sent, those whom the new world order did not consider worthy of trying to convert to the new system. Lenina agrees to go, but when Bernard asks for vacation time, his boss, the DHC, warns him that his curiosity and independent ways are not appreciated. The DHC warns him to mend his ways or else he will exile him to Iceland.

Bernard is shorter than most Alphas because a technician did not carefully monitor the test tube he was being developed in. But Bernard likes not being a clone of everyone else. He, personally, is eager to be independent in other ways, even though this is strongly discouraged by the state.

In Arizona, Bernard and Lenina meet a savage named John who was "born" by natural childbirth on the reservation. The thought of this makes Lenina sick but fascinates Bernard. He meets John's mother, Linda, and discovers that she used to live in Utopia until her boyfriend brought her to the reservation years ago, had sex with her until she became pregnant, then deserted her before their child (John) was born. Her former boyfriend, it turns out, is the DHC, boss of Bernard and Lenina.

Bernard asks to bring John the savage and his mother back to Utopia for further study. Mustapha Mond, the Controller of Western Europe, grants his request. Bernard brings back John and Linda and uses them to expose the DHC's past and to disgrace him. Suddenly, Bernard is a celebrity: He has toppled the DHC, and he is guardian of the curious savage. Women fall at his feet and seek to have sex and *soma* orgies with him. Bernard no longer wants to be different; he likes being part of the state if this is what it has to offer him.

Linda, now back in Utopia, swallows huge amounts of *soma* and goes on a blissful mind trip. John, however, is not impressed with Utopia. Back on the reservation, he had learned to read Shakespeare, but here the lower-class people have no hope of advancement.

Lenina is sexually aroused by John. She takes him to see a *feely*, a movie that provides visual, tactile, and olfactory sensations. She then takes him back to her apartment for sex, but John makes no attempt to seduce her. He bids her good night and leaves. Lenina swallows *soma* to cope with her frustration.

In time, John refuses to be put on display by Bernard any longer. Bernard loses his prestige and his lovers because of this. He no longer has status. He swallows *soma* to help him cope. Meanwhile, Lenina takes up with one of her former lovers, the Arch-

Community-Songster (of Canterbury), but she still sexually craves John the savage.

John and Bernard become friends again, and they visit Helmholtz Watson, a writer of Utopian propaganda who is now in trouble for teaching poetry to students. John recites Shakespearean poetry to Helmholtz, who particularly likes lines from *Romeo and Juliet*.

John realizes that he has been in love with Lenina for a long time. When she next comes to his apartment, he approaches her in the courtly fashion he has learned from Shakespeare's plays. She shocks him by stripping off all of her clothes and begging him to engage in frantic sex with her. He rejects her offer of sex and, instead, offers to marry her so that they can live together and start a family. This nauseates Lenina. Both leave the apartment totally perplexed by what the other has done.

John is summoned by telephone to the Hospital of the Dying, where he finds children observing his mother as she lies on a bed, ready to die. The children are watching so that they can be "death conditioned," but John chases them away. Linda then dies.

John, Bernard, and Helmholtz meet with Mustapha Mond. John and Helmholtz argue that Shakespeare is better than the feelies and that propaganda sayings are for mindless morons. Mustapha agrees but reminds them that eight-ninths of the population is created as laborers, so they wouldn't understand Shakespeare even if they had his works. Bernard sees that the meeting is not going well. He apologizes for his former independent ways and pleads with Mond for mercy. Mond cannot allow exceptions. He orders Bernard to be exiled to Iceland and Helmholtz to the Falkland Islands near Argentina.

Mustapha Mond still hopes to convert John, but the savage tells Mond that art and science are too much to give up in exchange for utopian living. Mond reminds him that even God has been given up. In a society that needs no favors or forgiveness or commiseration, God is unnecessary. *Soma*, he says, is Christianity without self-denial or chastity or guilt of sin.

John argues that a neutral life is so bland, it is worthless. He insists he would rather live with the problems of fear, hunger, old age, and pain rather than go through a dull and predictable existence.

John runs away and hides in Surrey, in a deserted lighthouse. He spends time hunting, planting, and praying. Soon, reporters locate him and pester him for statements. John takes a whip and beats himself to drive out thoughts of utopian ways. Cameramen film him and make a feely of the event. Thereafter, hundreds of people flock to the lighthouse and chant for John to show them how he whips himself. Lenina arrives by helicopter and calls to him, but he cannot hear what she is saying over the noise of the crowd. John rushes at her and begins to whip himself and Lenina. This makes the crowd go delirious. Soon, everyone—including John the savage—begins to take drugs and have a wild sex orgy.

Hours later, when John wakes up, he realizes he has been seduced by Utopia. He hates what he has become. He decides to exercise the one power of self-determination he has left. He kills himself.

So ends the novel . . . and so begins the debate over Huxley's eleven insights:

1. His *soma* predated our current need for a Drug Enforcement Agency to control the multibillion-dollar illegal narcotics problem in America.
2. His mind control by sleep training predated our laws against subliminal advertising in movies and on TV.
3. His test-tube assembly line predated our current gene splicing, DNA and RNA manipulating, and genetic engineering.
4. His population control predated our legalization of abortion and the Kevorkian court cases to legalize assisted suicides.

5. His savage wilderness in New Mexico predated our concerns over what to do about
   race riots.
6. His use of repetitive, nonproductive activities as a way of entertaining people predated
   our video games.
7. His "feelies" predated our movies with
   Dolby Sound, Cine-Rama, Surround Sound,
   Digitally Enhanced Imaging, and Techni-
   color.
8. His Ten World Controllers predated the establishment of the United Nations.
9. His prediction of rocket travel between continents predated the SST and Concorde.
10. His nuclear-free world predated our con-
    cerns about how to dispose of nuclear waste
    and how to defuse potential nuclear war.
11. His concept of random sex predated the Free
    Love movement of the 1960s, the Open Mar-
    riage concept of the 1970s, and the Gay
    Rights movement of the 1980s.

In the 1930s, people were stunned by Huxley's predictions. Today, readers are intrigued by how accurately he envisioned the developments of the coming
decades. The most interesting factor in all this, however, is how Huxley, himself, viewed his work. Quite
frankly, it saddened and horrified him that people did
not read his book and determine that this was *not* the
way society should continue. Fifteen years after the
publication of *Brave New World*, Huxley was asked to
write an introduction to a new printing of the novel.
He wrote, "[Back] then, I projected this six hundred
years into the future. Today it seems quite possible
that the horror may be upon us in a single century."
Thus, what we of the coming new millennium call
progress, Huxley called horror. His science fiction has,
in many ways, become our reality.

Maybe, as John the savage would suggest, it may

be time for us to turn back again to poetry, Shakespeare, and the pure forms of art and science.

1984 BY GEORGE ORWELL (1949)

It has been said that of the demons that drive a writer to write, none are more powerful than the bad experiences of the writer's own life. Certainly this was true of George Orwell. The characters in his novel *1984* experienced loneliness, hunger, poverty, sexual frustration, physical ailments, political upheaval, and class snobbery—all of which Orwell, himself, knew firsthand.

Orwell's real name was Eric Blair. He was born in 1903 in India, where his father was a lowly British official. Eric's father sent the family back to England, and at age eight Eric began living at St. Cyprian's boarding school. He attended on a scholarship, which made him "lower class" in the eyes of the other students. Later, at Eton, also on scholarship, he remained an outsider. He turned to writing poetry and reporting for school publications as creative outlets. He also read avidly and was greatly moved by two works of Jack London: the socialist novel *The Iron Heel* and the sociological study *The People of the Abyss*. The latter found Jack London living as a derelict among the street people in the worst sections of London, England, and then writing a book (with photographs) about their plight.

Without money to attend college, young Eric Blair enlisted for five years of service as a British policeman in Burma. He detested the job, not only because it took him so far away from home and family, but also because it put him in the role of imperialist law enforcer over weak, uneducated people. His health failed; he returned to England and resigned his position.

Emulating his literary hero, Jack London, Eric put

on tattered clothing and lived among the destitute people of France and England until he developed pneumonia and nearly died in the paupers' wing of a French hospital. He came home and chronicled his experiences in *Down and Out in Paris and London*, publishing the book under the pen name of George Orwell to spare his family any embarrassment.

Blair married in 1935 but was always restless. In 1936, he lived among the coal miners of northern England and became a socialist in the process. His book *The Road to Wigan Pier* recorded this experience. He next started writing novels, but with modest success. Later, he served in Spain with the freedom fighters who were resisting Franco, but he was shot by a sniper and came home wounded and defeated. He then turned his pen to attacking totalitarian governments, continuing to write as George Orwell.

In 1945, Orwell's fantasy satire, *Animal Farm*, brought him world fame, but shortly thereafter he developed tuberculosis and became very weak. Rather than recuperate in a clinic, he stayed at home for the next two years, writing *1984*. It was published to rave reviews in 1949, but the ordeal of writing it proved too taxing for Orwell. He died at age forty-seven in 1950.

Although Orwell's *1984* had marvelous elements of science fiction—most notably, the accurate prediction of in-home wide screen televisions, global news reporting by newsreel, and the development of atomic arsenals—it was its accurate predictions of political and societal developments that made it a controversial book (remaining so even after 1984 came and went).

The novel's central character is Winston Smith, whose occupation involves rewriting history so as to make the government of INGSOC (English Socialism) and its nebulous leader, Big Brother, always seem correct in all of their actions and decisions. Though considered unthinkable in Orwell's day, this is common practice today. Filmmaker Oliver Stone has had great success with movies such as *JFK* and *Nixon*, which contain fabricated history created for dramatic effect; and prior to the fall of the U.S.S.R., that nation was constantly rewriting its history (Stalin the savior . . . Stalin the butcher). Orwell's fiction has long since become our reality.

The novel presents two classes of people. The Proles (for "proletariats") are the outcast, uneducated common folk who live and breed in the bombed-out slum areas of London. Their favorite pastimes are buying lottery tickets and drinking liquor. Interestingly, the U.S. in the years since *1984* was published temporarily lowered its legal drinking age to eighteen in nearly every state, and most states now have a government-run series of lotteries. (Coincidence or inevitable trend?)

A more privileged class of people are the government workers like Winston Smith. They live in better housing but are watched by two-way TV monitors and are brainwashed regularly with sayings such as FREEDOM IS SLAVERY . . . WAR IS PEACE . . . IGNORANCE IS STRENGTH. The party's slogan is "Who controls the past controls the future; who controls the present controls the past."

Smith is depressed by the world he finds himself in. He secretly begins to rebel: He keeps a daily journal in which he admits that he hates Big Brother and the government he represents; he goes among the Proles in search of clues about the way life was before the revolution; and he rents a secluded apartment where he meets his lover, Julia, who also is a government worker who dislikes the current system.

All citizens fear the Thought Police, who are assigned to track down dissidents and either kill them or take them to the dreaded Ministry of Love for reprogramming. However, rumor has it that an underground movement has been formed to overthrow the current government. Winston Smith suspects that a man named O'Brien, a member of the government's Inner Party, may really be a leader in the underground. Smith dreams of O'Brien coming to recruit him.

In the end, O'Brien does recruit Smith. He brings Smith and his girlfriend, Julia, to his luxurious home and even gives Smith a book written by Goldstein, the mythic hero of the underground. Goldstein's book explains how Big Brother and INGSOC were developed, the weaknesses in the system, and the results of letting it continue. Smith is fascinated, but Julia (a pragmatist) does not care who is in control of the government so long as she can sneak some extra goods for herself and continue to see Winston Smith.

Back at their secret apartment, the Thought Police burst in on Winston and Julia. A poster falls from the wall to reveal a two-way television that has been watching them all along. The man who rented them the apartment is an informer, and O'Brien is not really a traitor to Big Brother.

Smith is imprisoned in the Ministry of Love for months. He is given shock treatments; he is starved; he is whipped and clubbed; he is even strapped down and put into a cage where rats nibble at his face. Finally, he cracks. He tells O'Brien anything the man wants to hear ("Two and two are five" ... "War is peace") and he even denounces Julia, his lover.

Having been reprogrammed, Smith is released to live among the Proles. His hair is gray, many of his teeth are missing, he has lost weight [perhaps an image of Orwell himself in the final stages of TB], and he is weak. By chance, he meets Julia. She is now bloated, wrinkled, and pale. He confesses that he denied her; she, likewise, tells him she denounced him. They go their separate ways. Smith wanders into a bar and sits among the other broken souls. When the image of Big Brother comes on television, Smith smiles in euphoric peace. He loves Big Brother. His reconditioning has been perfected.

In the analysis of *1984*, it is obvious that aspects of recent history were incorporated by Orwell, most notably in the way the Thought Police resemble Hitler's

Gestapo and how the rewriting of history was not dissimilar from the World War II practice of reporting only battle victories. However, other elements were contemporary, such as the use of shock therapy for altering brain conditions, which was a new theory in Orwell's day. And still other elements were futuristic, such as the brainwashing that would be developed during the Korean War, the use of television to mold public opinion, and the development of an atomic bomb that could be delivered against an enemy via a missile.

If Orwell was a prophet of doom, he was nevertheless accurate in many of his predictions. Those who read *1984* today do not say that the year came and went and Orwell missed his call; they say, instead, that he may have missed the date, but he foresaw the inevitable.

One fact becomes obvious upon examination of the information in this chapter: People have always been —interested in the future. What's more, they have been willing to pay for other people's speculations about the future. In ancient times, people turned to soothsayers, mystics, astrologers, and seers for predictions. Today, we turn to economic forecasters, sports games oddsmakers, and television weather announcers for insights on what the morrow will bring. We are no different today from folks of previous generations. And because of that, the utopian novel is destined to remain a mainstay in literary offerings.

Literary dreamers have the dual ability to teach us while entertaining us. They cause us to consider where we have been and to contemplate where we are going. They often scare us; but, in so doing, they also give us perspective.

That, easily, justifies the cost of a novel.

3: Religious Views of the New World Order

BYRON AND Annie Kirkwood live in the Ozark foothills of northeast Oklahoma. They are the spiritual leaders of a group calling itself the Earth Changers. According to the Kirkwoods, if mankind does not get right with the planet Earth—soon!—the coming millennium will mean the end of civilization.

With religious zeal, the Kirkwoods proclaim to their followers (and to any media personnel who will give them coverage) that Earth is using tornadoes, floods, earthquakes, landslides, blizzards, volcanoes, and even diseases such as AIDS to rid itself of humans. They believe, however, that people can escape the impending doom by learning to live in peace and harmony.

Although referring to themselves as spiritual leaders, the Kirkwoods are considered by certain critics to be opportunists. Byron has written a self-published book titled *Survival Guide for the New Millennium.* He also happens to be a vendor of "Spiritual Advancement and Emergency Preparedness Products," which include nitrogen-packed, long-shelf-life foods, miners' hard hats, solar-powered radios, respirators, flashlights, waterproof matches, flares, canteens, tents, and first aid kits. Besides selling products to his followers, Byron also mails a monthly newsletter to Earth

Changers who live in at least thirty different states of the union.

Whether referred to as futurists or isolationists or religious fanatics, groups such as the Earth Changers seem to be proliferating as the countdown draws closer to the arrival of the new millennium. Often they are small sects, seeking privacy and spiritual harmony with the world as they prepare for life in the next millennium; other times, however, they are extremists, such as the thirty-nine members of the Heaven's Gate (aka Higher Source) cult who committed group suicide in March 1997 at the California home they rented for communal living.

In the United States, the decade of the 1990s has seen the flourishing of more than five-thousand cults, many of which are concentrating their energies on proclaiming a message of doom and destruction for the next millennium. A quick overview of this decade shows a long list of cults that have chosen to act on their pessimism about the next millennium by committing mass suicides:

- A dozen people in Tijuana, Mexico, emulating the suicide pact of the followers of Jim Jones in Guyana (November 18, 1978), drank a mixture of industrial alcohol and orange juice on December 13, 1990, as part of a religious ritual. All twelve people died.
- David Koresh and eighty members of his Branch Davidian cult walled themselves inside a wooden complex near Waco, Texas, in early 1993 and used high-powered weapons to fend off anyone who came near them. After fifty-one days of a standoff involving the state and federal governments, the FBI engaged in a six-hour gun battle with the Dividians. In an effort to force the Dividians out of their stronghold, the FBI shot tear gas into the complex. Rather than surrender, the Dividians ignited their complex and burned themselves

(including eighteen youngsters) to death on April 19.

- A global cult known as the Order of the Solar Temple believes that humans are meant to live on Earth only for a short time and then should be transferred to a planet they refer to as "Sirius." However, the only way that humans can go through this transition is by observing a religious ritual that involves lining themselves up in a star pattern on a floor and then setting fire to the building they are in as an act of mass suicide. For a fact, members of this cult have followed through on this ritual on numerous occasions. On March 22, 1997, five members of Solar Temple burned themselves to death in a fire in St. Casimir, Quebec, Canada. Previously, on December 23, 1995, sixteen members of Solar Temple burned themselves to death in a little house in Grenoble, France. Before that, forty-eight members of Solar Temple killed themselves in fires in Switzerland, and five members killed themselves in Morin Heights (near Montreal), Canada, in late 1994.
- When the thirty-nine members of the Heaven's Gate cult committed mass suicide in a complex near San Diego in March 1997, they left videotapes and journals which explained that they were killing themselves in order to rendezvous with an alien space vehicle that was flying in the wake of the Hale-Bopp comet. For some reason, the cult members prepared themselves by shaving their heads, dressing in black clothes and Nike tennis shoes, and lying faceup in bunk beds.

If fringe religious groups and suicide cults seem to be getting most of the press play these days, that is not to say that the mainline religious groups are not also focusing their attention on the new millennium.

Many of them are coordinating efforts to present their messages, advance their agendas, and promote their beliefs.

BUDDHISM

Founded in 525 B.C. by Siddhārtha Gautama (563–483 B.C.) near Benares, India, Buddhism is a dominant religion throughout Japan and much of Asia. It also has an estimated 800,000 followers in the United States. It is founded on the belief that life has no ultimate meaning and that all living beings are in a state of decay. Through reincarnation, a person's spirit can be born and reborn in never-ending cycles until one is able to develop a mental discipline that will allow him or her to reach Nirvana, a state of nothingness that supersedes the existent "self."

Tenzin Gyatso, the fourteenth Dalai Lama (now in exile, though still considered the spiritual leader of Tibet), is an optimistic leader of the Buddhist people. This is ironic to a point, for Buddhists are pessimists by nature and have never shown much interest in futurism other than to wonder what form they would return in after their deaths. Gyatso, himself, has said he never worries about what people will think of him when he is gone, but is far more concerned about what he can be doing at present to use his time profitably for the benefit of other people.

When asked by interviewer Claudia Dreifus what religion will be like after the new millennium, if nature has been damaged, the Dalai Lama replied, "The world itself is nature. The sun, the moon, they are nature. Even if there were no more animals, nature would still be there. For those religions that believe in a creator, they would have to find reasons to explain why our beautiful blue planet became a desert. If you ask me if it's good or bad, of course it's bad. But in the Buddhist tradition, something like that would not change our attitude. We believe the whole world will come and disappear, come and disappear—so, eventually the world becomes desert and even the ocean dries up. But then again, another new world is reborn. It's endless." (*The New York Times Magazine*, September 29, 1996, p. 168.)

JEHOVAH'S WITNESSES

Founded in 1870 by a former Presbyterian named Charles Taze Russell, the Jehovah's Witnesses now claim 4.5 million members. The denomination was formally incorporated in 1884 as the Watch Tower Bible and Tract Society of Pennsylvania. The name Jehovah's Witnesses did not come into popular use until the 1930s.

Of all the Bible-based Christian denominations, only the Jehovah's Witnesses have gone on record with a prediction of when the world will end in the apocalyptic holocaust forecast in the book of Revelation. Based on a complicated series of mathematical equations drawn from various references in the Bible, founder Charles Taze Russell predicted that Jesus would return to Earth in his second coming in 1914. At that time, there would be 144,000 witnesses (as explained in Revelation, in its discussion of the original twelve Jewish tribes) who would be called upon to reign from heaven as priests and kings over a new "kingdom of God on Earth." Many other people would be saved during this time and, subsequently, would live eternally in heaven with God.

When the year 1914 came and went without the world coming to an end, the leadership of the Jehovah's Witnesses announced that Jesus, indeed, had returned to Earth in 1914, but that he had been invisible. They then announced that Matthew 24:34 in the New Testament, which refers to a generation that would not pass away before the world's end, was being fulfilled starting in a countdown from 1914. Thus, when all people born during or before 1914 have died, the apocalypse will occur. Since the year 2000 will mark the passing of eighty-six years since the 1914 prediction (with the average life span of most people being about seventy-four years), many Jehovah's Witnesses believe that the new millennium will surely mark the end of time.

However, not all of the members believe this. Some, such as former governing-board member Raymond Franz, have speculated, "They'll have to make some kind of change. It's becoming absolutely untenable." (*U.S. News & World Report*, June 13, 1994, p. 76.)

With the year 2000 fast approaching, and fewer and fewer people remaining alive from the year 1914, the faithful among the Jehovah's Witnesses are looking skyward. For many members of this denomination, the arrival time of their messiah is at hand.

JUDAISM

Jews hold a unique position in religious orders in that they believe they are God's "chosen people," set apart for special blessing and strict justice directly from the Almighty . . . and, interestingly, many of the other religious sects believe this about the Jews as well. Most conservative Protestants, particularly the Baptists, recognize the Jews as a nation of people who have been "set apart by God" for divine ruling.

Where these groups differ, however, is in what they believe the outcome of this divine attention will be. For the Jews, it is a belief that there is yet to come a messiah who will bring peace and wisdom to the world. For non-Jews, it is a belief that the Jews have rejected the messiah who has already come—Jesus—thus causing continuous judgment to fall upon them as a people.

The coming of the third millennium since Christ

holds no special significance for Jews. They date time from biblical creation; thus, the year 2000 will be the year 5760 on the Jewish calendar and, as such, of no special importance.

Nevertheless, small cell groups within the larger realm of Judaism are of interest to futurists. Some rabbis have said they believe the messiah they have long awaited will come 240 years from now. Other Jews (Hasidic) previously proclaimed Rabbi Menachem Schneerson of Brooklyn, New York, to be that messiah, and they faithfully followed his teachings and leadership for more than forty years, even when at age ninety-two he could no longer speak or walk due to two paralyzing strokes. And, in Israel itself, there is a group of conservative Jews known as *Ateret Hacohanim* that is so sure the messiah's coming is pending, they are studying and practicing the ancient laws of animal sacrifice; once the messiah returns and rebuilds the Temple of Solomon, these Jews will be prepared to provide proper homage to him.

So it is, then, that even an ancient order like Judaism is not immune to those of their number who would predict what the future holds for members of their sect. They have tradition on their side. Many of the Old Testament prophets, especially Daniel and Isaiah, made predictions of what the "end times" would be like.

CATHOLICISM

In 1516, the Fifth Lateran Council for the Catholic church went on record as saying that all efforts to predict the date of the second coming of Christ, the coming of the Antichrist, or the end of the world should be avoided.

In an article printed in the *National Catholic Reporter* (August 11, 1995), writer Joseph Gallagher wrote, "There is absolutely no biblical reason to suppose that the coming of a new millennium has any special theological/biblical significance. From the scriptural point of view, the disputed question is whether there will be a peaceful 1,000-year period after the defeat of the Antichrist and the chaining of Satan, and before the world ends with Satan's final defeat. The biblical 'millennium' has nothing to do with the arrival of the new calendar 'millennium.' "

These disclaimers aside, the Catholic church is very interested in the next millennium. It sees the year 2000 as the bimillennium jubilee of Christ's birth and, thus, a cause for celebration that honors the birth that occurred in Bethlehem. The way this jubilee will be celebrated will be a parallel to the way the Old Testament described the setting aside of every seventh year for a jubilee year—slaves were freed, debts were forgiven, captives were released, poverty was eliminated among neighbors. Additionally, the mission of Jesus, as explained in Luke 4:18-19, to preach the good news to the poor and to set at liberty those who are oppressed, will also be copied. The specific ways this will be carried out by Catholics will be through global promotion of religious freedom, ecumenism, dialogue among various religions, and world evangelism.

As to evangelism, the Pope has reminded Catholics of the mandate of I Corinthians 9:16, which states, "Woe to me if I do not preach the Gospel." For the Catholic church, this now includes a burden to re-evangelize the traditionally Christian nations of the West that are now declining in church attendance, membership, and practices of worship.

The Pope was quoted in *America* magazine (December 9, 1995, p. 11) as explaining, "God is opening before the church the horizons of humanity more fully prepared for the sowing of the Gospel. I sense that the moment has come to commit all of the church's energies to a new evangelism and to the mission *ad gentes*. No believer in Christ, no institution of the church can avoid this supreme duty: to proclaim Christ to all peoples."

In line with this, the Pope has called on all churches—Roman Catholic, Eastern Orthodox, and Protestant—that proclaim Christ as their Lord to unite in "the promotion of fitting ecumenical initiatives so that we can celebrate the Great Jubilee, if not completely united, at least much closer to overcoming the divisions of the second millennium." (ibid.) To achieve this, the Pope is asking for theological dialogues wherein differences can be diminished and churches can accept each other's members in harmony.

This appeal has fallen on deaf ears, for the most part, in the Protestant community. However, a few highly visible leaders among Protestant groups, such as former Watergate conspirator turned Christian author and prison evangelist Charles Colson, have said publicly that Catholics and Protestants should make a mutual effort to project a united front for evangelism in the next millennium. Certain Protestants, however, continue to point out that many of the Catholic practices, such as praying to saints rather than to Christ, bowing before statues, and being absolved by priests for sins rather than being absolved by Christ, are in direct violation of the tenets of their faith and, as such, prevent them from affiliating spiritually with Catholics.

The Pope also has a political agenda. In speaking before the United Nations on October 5, 1995, and in material published in his book *Crossing the Threshold of Hope* (1994), the Pope has said that he believes, following in the custom of the Old Testament celebration of the jubilee year, nations should forgive the debts of other nations; in fact, the world governments should work to eliminate the global debt entirely.

Furthermore, the church's agenda for the next millennium should be, in many instances, to make restitution and pay penance and seek reconciliation for past wrongs of this current millennium. Although the

Pope has not been specific in explaining what these past wrongs might be, observers have pointed out that many members of the Catholic church now feel that the barbaric acts during the Inquisition, the battles fought during the Crusades, the tolerance shown for slavery on numerous continents, and the lack of a stronger stance against the persecution of Jews are deeds all Christians must feel ashamed about. In writing to the Fourth World Congress on Women, held in China in September 1995, the Pope also sent a letter apologizing on behalf of the church for any lack of respect for women that may have been shown in previous centuries.

It is the intent of the Pope to make every possible effort to visit Jerusalem and the Holy Lands during the year 2000. By going to Bethlehem, Damascus, Mount Sinai, the Sea of Galilee, and other Old and New Testament places of historical significance, the Pope hopes to open dialogues with leaders of the Jewish, Muslim, and Christian faiths. In this effort, the new millennium may be a time of mutual harmony and spiritual cooperation, as opposed to the bygone eras of conflict and adversarial infighting.

DIVIDED WE FALL

If the Catholic church has high ideals and grand goals for the coming millennium, it also has internal deterioration. And in that, it is not unlike other sects, churches, denominations, and religions.

In his 1997 book titled *The Empty Church*, Episcopalian researcher Prof. Thomas C. Reeves has presented some startling facts about the public's lack of interest in mainline churches during the close of the twentieth century. He reports that in 1985, 33 percent of the Methodist churches performed no baptisms. In the Methodist church, Presbyterian church, and Episcopalian church, only half the young people of families of those denominations have chosen to remain in the denomination after they have come of age (and 48 percent of Presbyterian youth never return to *any* church). At present, 60 percent of American teenagers don't know that it was Jesus who delivered the Sermon on the Mount, and 70 percent of American teenagers, when asked to explain the religious significance of Easter, were unable to do so. Furthermore, 30 percent of all Americans say they have a totally secular outlook on life, 29 percent say they are "nominally religious," 22 percent say they are "modestly religious," and only 19 percent (about 36 million people) say they seriously follow the dictates and beliefs of their faith and are actively involved in worship.

In spite of these statistics, Reeves points out that in a 1994 exit poll survey conducted during the presidential election, 56 percent of Americans said that the problems facing the nation were "primarily moral and social" in nature, and 65 percent of these voters said they would be more apt to support a candidate whose party's top priority was to reverse the moral decline in the country. In a nation where 30 percent of all births are illegitimate, and illegal drug use and crime are on the rise, Reeves gives a nod of understanding.

Research reported by Tom Roberts in *National Catholic Reporter* (January 13, 1995) showed that, despite the fact that Catholics are mandated to be faithful in church attendance each week, only 28 percent are actually attending on a regular basis. Citing a study done by two Notre Dame University researchers, Mark Chaves and James Cavendish, Roberts reported statistics that showed that, compared to the populations of a given sect in specific areas of the country, only 20 percent of people calling themselves Protestant were attending church and only 28 percent of people labeling themselves Catholic were attending church.

These numbers came as a great shock to many leaders of the Catholic church who, for years, had cited the Gallup Poll, which had claimed that 51 percent of all Catholics and 45 percent of all Protestants attended church on a regular basis. The Gallup Poll, however, was done by calling people on the telephone and asking them how often they attended church. These people often exaggerated their church attendance so as to sound "proper." Chaves and Cavendish, though, actually went to the churches and counted heads and compared those numbers to the number of people who were members of a given church. In conducting research in 48 of the 174 territorial dioceses in the continental United States, it was shown that church attendance showed an average absentee rate of 72 percent.

But if attendance at traditional mainline churches is falling off, does this mean a lack of interest or, instead, a turning of interest in new directions? Some researchers claim it is the latter.

J. Gordon Melton, chief researcher and editor of the *Encyclopedia of American Religions*, noted in *U.S. Catholic* (September 1994, p.35) that there are from five hundred to six hundred "nonconventional denominations" in America at present. Unlike Ireland, India, and Bosnia, where religious differences are cause for unending war, America seems to have developed a spiritual elasticity that has permitted virtually any sect or denomination to get a foothold in this country. America now has approximately 1,515 Buddhist temples, 1,139 Muslim mosques, and 412 Hindu houses of worship. Because so much of America's black population has embraced the Islamic faith, it now is almost equal in numbers to the Jewish followers in the United States.

Such diversity does present its problems, too. In trying to decide what are the rights of religious freedom, state and federal government agencies have been caught in a legal and religious cross fire. Prisoners in New Jersey and Georgia have asked to worship on Fridays because they are Muslims. Orthodox Jews serving as rabbis in the military have asked to violate Air Force dress regulations in order to wear a skullcap. Sikhs serving in the military have petitioned to be allowed to grow their beards, for their faith forbids shaving them. Muslim women in four states have sought an exception to revealing their faces for driver's license photos since wearing a veil is part of their religious discipline.

A question then arises as to whether or not both the government and churches will have to adapt so as to reflect the needs and desires of the people they serve. There is significant evidence this has already begun to occur.

Martin E. Marty, reporting in *The Christian Century* (January 15, 1997), cited research conducted by Benton Johnson of the University of Oregon. Johnson led a study in 1962 that showed that conservative Protestants believed social dancing, drinking alcohol, gambling, and filing for divorce were terrible sins; and, to that end, pastors devoted the majority of their sermons to denouncing these practices.

However, only a quarter of a century later, because the customs of the people attending churches had changed so radically so as to accept these practices, the frequency of sermons against such practices decreased significantly. For example, in 1962, more than 80 percent of the Baptist pastors surveyed had preached a sermon against alcohol that year; in 1987, only 24 percent had done so. In 1987, 92 percent of the Southern Baptist preachers had preached a sermon denouncing social dancing, but by 1987, only 13 percent had done so. In 1962, only one state in the union (Nevada) permitted legalized gambling; by 1997, forty-eight states not only permitted it, but many of them were directly promoting it through state lotteries. Times changed, people changed, and, apparently, so did the emphasis of sermon topics.

In many areas of spiritual disciplines, a movement toward liberal thinking has permeated the conservative churches. The emphasis on women being "the weaker vessel" and being submissive to their hus-

band as been replaced by a focus on equality of the
sexe he unwritten law that no work or shopping
sho   be done on Sundays has been replaced by a
beli at as long as one finds time to worship some-
time during the week, it will be just as valid as on a
Sunday.

Not all areas have shown changes, however. There
is still strong opposition among conservative churches
in regard to smoking tobacco or using illegal drugs or
aborting children. And, in some churches, there is evidence of some holding fast to the other firm beliefs.
This has led to a dividing of the camp, with members
of the same congregation often finding themselves on
opposite ends of an issue.

Certain members of the clergy are encouraged by
such occurrences. They feel that when people leave
the church because they cannot identify with what is
being taught or what is being shared, the lost congre-
gationalist suffers as well as the church as a whole.
Better, they feel, would it be to have the church learn
how to minister to the current needs of such people
than to ridicule or upbraid them.

Other members of the clergy scoff at such tolerance,
saying that religious discipline is part of the ritual of
showing faith in God and honor to his laws, cove-
nants, and mandates. If religion can mean anything
anyone wants it to mean, the church serves no purpose other than to assuage people's consciences and
to provide a building for socializing. No sincere relationship with God can be developed.

No Radical New World Order

So it is, then, that we find that specific religious
orders are looking toward the year 2000 as a time of
major upheaval in the religious world order. They are
preparing for it by planning ways to celebrate it . . .
or to counteract it.

In reality, however, whereas small sects and cults are gaining national headlines with certain outlandish practices, for the most part the mainline religions are doing what they can to maintain "the flock" and respond to contemporary issues. As a nation, America professes its need for greater social and moral discipline, while, at the same time, its people aren't bothering to fill the pews as often as in days gone by.

History shows that the pendulum can swing back to revival and conservatism, as evidenced during the Victorian era; however, there seems to be no immediate evidence of such an occurrence pending. And, if not, there are plenty of advocates of an end-of-the-world apocalyptic bent who will proclaim, "The end is near."

Only time, itself, will reveal who is right.

4: The Six Waves of Economic Change

In 1976, Dr. Alvin Toffler was touring the country giving lectures based on research he had presented in his best-selling book *Future Shock*. The premise of his book was that the future had come so rapidly—major advances in technology, space exploration, educational theories, and medical breakthroughs—that no one entering the decade of the 1970s had been prepared to cope with such great changes in their lives. As such, they had experienced (and were continuing to experience) sensation overload. It was leaving them numb, in a state of societal shock. In effect, the future had proved to be too phenomenal for the average human being to handle.

Interestingly enough, Toffler's book of two decades ago now seems bland, for although it made an earnest effort to present the rapid changes of the current and forthcoming years, it made no mention of most of the things that today are most vital in our lives. For example, it mentioned nothing about DNA splicing and cell cloning, silicon chips, VCRs or Betamax, cellular phones or call waiting, MTV, NutraSweet, Prozac, rap music, E-mail, the World Wide Web or the Internet, airline frequent flyer programs, Nintendo or Sega or Gameboy or Atari, Macintosh computers, the X-Men or Mighty Morphin Power Rangers or the Teenage Mutant Ninja Turtles, Express Mail, *USA Today*, Nautilus or StairMaster exercise equipment, laser discs or CD-ROM.

Additionally, Toffler gave no indication that such major changes in the business and political realms were pending as the fall of the Berlin Wall and the breakup of the U.S.S.R., the end of white rule in South Africa, the reinstituting of relations between the U.S. and Vietnam, the worldwide epidemic of AIDS, the assassinations of Anwar Sadat (1981) and Yitzhak Rabin (1995), the disbanding of AT&T, or U.S. troops taking aggressive action with the United Nations in Kuwait (1990) and later Bosnia (1996).

If today we were to accept Toffler's measuring stick for intake overload and, thus, agree that people were in a state of "future shock" in 1975, it would mean that by today's standards, folks would have to be completely blotto. Things are moving ten times faster in the late 1990s than they were in 1975.

People aren't blotto, however. Nor are they numb or in shock. For a fact, the current generation has virtually gone in the other direction. Since so many amazing changes have come about in so short a time, very little seems to dazzle people today. Instead of being in shock, they are blasé and nonchalant about many of the current breakthroughs. In fact, if there is a reaction at all these days, it is usually either *anger* over the "slowness" of progress ("Why haven't they found a cure for AIDS yet?") or *distrust* of those people who seem to have influence in shaping the future ("This darn computer system was obsolete six months after I bought it. Why didn't they warn me about that when I bought it!").

Without being intimidated by the future, the current generation is coming to expect material goods that are faster, more accurate, lower priced, more durable, less complicated, and more eye-appealing than anything ever previously produced. And on one hand, they aren't being disappointed. Such materials are being developed, mass-produced, distributed, and advertised and marketed on a continuing basis.

On the other hand, however, there is a serious glitch in the system. Whereas members of the younger generation are eager to have products and services at new levels of efficiency, they do not have the available cash to buy such niceties. People of this era have been labeled "Generation X" because of the symbolic crossed-out mark that has been drawn over their chance to exceed the successes of their parents.

"My great-grandfather started working in the automobile factories here in Detroit, when old Henry Ford himself was still running things," explains Mike, a twenty-three-year-old unemployed laborer in Michigan.

"When the unions were organized, our family had an inside track to membership. My great-grandfather got my grandfather in, my grandfather got my dad in . . . and I just assumed that my dad would get me in. And he would have, if there'd been any jobs available. Trouble is, what used to take eighteen or twenty men to accomplish is now being done by one man, a computer, and two robots. I didn't even bother to earn my high school diploma. I just assumed I'd step into a fifteen-dollar-an-hour union job, with benefits, and I'd be set for life. It didn't work out that way, though. I'm now working the afternoon shift at a car wash."

Mike is representative of many people of his generation. The long-held belief of parents that "my kid's gonna have it better than me" no longer applies. For a fact, due to massive layoffs brought about by reengineering, downsizing, computerizing, and roboticizing, many of the parents are now more worried about hanging onto their own jobs than worrying about where the next generation is going to find employment.

So it is, then, that Generation X is fully ready to accept whatever material changes the future wishes to provide as a better way of life; however, Generation X is simultaneously being made obsolete as a workforce by many of the systems being developed to produce these marvelous goods and materials.

"This scenario is the result of raising a generation of young people who were given many material benefits," explains Roger Herman, "yet who were not simultaneously told that the free ride was quickly coming to an end."

Herman, author of *Turbulence! Challenges and Opportunities in the World of Work* (Oakhill Press, 1995), explains, "Many people today who have minimal skills are either on welfare or are working minimum-wage jobs at fast-food restaurants or department stores. Their money comes hard, so they are tight-fisted with it. They are steadily putting demands on retailers to make the 'good life' available to them at an affordable price. This is not easy, because the research and development costs for newer and better products drives the selling price up. It's rough going both for the Generation X customer and the retailer."

Roger Herman and other business futurists agree that, in the end, it's the pursuit of the dollar that will determine all economic developments. Understanding that, we can see some very specific patterns shaping the future. Six such developments are rolling toward us like the waves of a pounding surf.

START PADDLING, SURF'S UP!

To understand the coming changes in the ever-altering economy, we'll liken such changes to the waves of the ocean. The surfers trying to ride these economic waves are the retailers.

An experienced surfer will take his surfboard and paddle far out into the ocean, sitting astride the board as though riding on horseback. Once the surfer is a mile or more away from shore, he will do an about-face and turn the board toward the land. He then will sit there, bobbing atop the water with his head turned over his shoulder, watching each wave as it rolls toward him.

Although dozens of small waves continuously move toward, then past the surfer, he has no interest in them. His eye is vigilantly scanning the horizon in search of a giant wave, a major swell, a huge curl with force and drive and power.

Finally, the surfer spots such a wave. He sees it coming toward him, gaining momentum as it churns onward, lifting and whirling, creating a mighty vortex of wind and undertow and forward rush. The surfer smiles. Yes! This is the ride of a lifetime. This is what he has been waiting and watching for, and if he can time it just right, it will carry him high and will transport him all the way to the distant shore.

Energetically, the surfer lies down on the board and begins to paddle his arms in powerful strokes. He must get "up to speed" before the wave arrives; otherwise, he will be crushed beneath the wall of water and snapped like a twig.

With a predetermined sense of direction and speed, the surfer puts his full effort into making his board race forward. Soon, he has it gliding rapidly, its nose knifing through the currents.

Then, suddenly, the wave is there, coming upon the surfer. The surfer times his standing motion so that he rises to the top of his board at the same time the board rises to the top of the wave. It is a marvelous harmony of motion, and it works perfectly.

From the shore, the onlookers gaze through binoculars and watch the majestic sight of the champion surfer as he rides the wave, always at the crest, always in control. The ride lasts for a long time and ends only when the surfer glides on the final momentum of the now-spent wave to the shallows of the shoreline. The onlookers applaud, marveling at the rider's ability to choose the right wave, to know when to get aboard, and to be able to stay on top for the entire ride.

Indeed, this is the very challenge now being faced by economic surfers. The smart ones are already paddling into very deep waters and are diligently and vigilantly watching for the coming big waves. Those who see them coming and paddle powerfully to be "up to speed" when they arrive, are ready to ride the new economic crest of prosperity. However, those who improperly time the waves will be washed over and crushed beneath them.

FIRST WAVE:
MOVING FROM STANDARD PRACTICES TO CONTINUOUS ADAPTABILITY

Prior to the decade of the 1990s, most business operations changed only cosmetically. One year, men's ties were wide; the next year, they were narrow. One year, women's hemlines were up; the next year, they were down. One year, cars had fins; the next year, they didn't. One year, boys wore hair over their ears; the next year, they were back to crew cuts. So it went: The styles changed, but the basic product or service stayed the same.

By the year 2000, this will no longer be true. By then, when changes are made, both the bathwater *and* the baby will be thrown out.

One evidence of this is the way coins and paper money are becoming obsolete. Electronic transfers of funds through credit cards are done today for everything from purchasing life insurance policies to making donations to the offering plate at church. To rent a car, you *must* have a credit card (cash is not acceptable). Many workers never see a paycheck; their salaries are automatically deposited into their bank accounts by their employers, and they then use debit cards to draw against the available balance for whatever shopping they need to do. The whole system of using actual cash-in-hand is rapidly being abandoned.

Similarly, the daily newspaper will soon become a thing of the past. For news, people will go to their personal computers at home. They will access E-mail or the Internet, and they will call up just the news they wish to read—football scores of class B high schools in the upper peninsula of Michigan; stock reports of undercapitalized diamond mines in Africa; voting results of the special election for a new senator in Utah; fashion news from the spring shows in Paris. Rather than wait for the news to happen, then wait for someone to write it, then wait for it to be typeset and printed, then wait for it to be delivered to their front doorstep, readers will access an electronic newspaper at their own convenience.

"But I can't imagine a world without cash or without a nightly newspaper," you may be protesting.

Nevertheless, this will be one of the keys to survival. Businesses that are flexible enough to abandon the status quo in favor of radical changes will find themselves surviving even amidst times of major economic upheaval.

"The reason flexibility will be so important to consumers," explains Edwin C. Leonard, Ph.D., "is because the two things consumers value most are ease of use and the saving of time. If companies can alter their previously set-in-stone ways of providing goods and services so as to meet these two criteria, they will maintain a strong customer base."

Dr. Leonard, a professor of business at Indiana University and coauthor of *Supervision: Concepts and Practices of Management* (6th ed., South-Western College Publishing, 1995), explains, "Look at how people already are becoming fanatics about trying to save time. They eat at drive-through restaurants, they use throwaway diapers for their babies, they hire lawn care services to fertilize their lawns, they buy home pregnancy tests rather than wait in a doctor's office, they listen to books on tape while driving, and they heat up thirty-second microwave snacks rather than cook."

Dr. Leonard notes that such personalized conveniences as on-command cable video movies, self-timed VCRs, and talking computers all point to a situation of flexibility in meeting customer needs.

"The point," says Dr. Leonard, "is that companies and service businesses must create systems that are flexible and able to respond to both environmental changes and customer trends."

One good example of this is the Honda Automotive Corporation of Japan. Previously, with American automobile manufacturers, a new line of cars would be presented once each year, usually around October. These cars would feature new accessories, new safety devices, and new stylistic designs. Honda, however, began to stop its assembly line each time it developed an innovative way to improve the performance of its cars. That modification was added immediately, not the following autumn at model changeover time. What this means is, the customer has always been getting the most up-to-date Honda possible, whether the vehicle was purchased in January, April, September, or any other month of the year.

Another prime example is the ordering process of shelf goods found at Wal-Mart. Previously, companies such as Sears would wait until they were low on certain products, and then they would place an order with the subsidiary or supplying company that manufactured that product. Quite often, if the delivery process required a lot of paperwork and preparation and shipping, the store might be "temporarily out" of the product.

Wal-Mart, however, has set up direct lines of purchase communication between its stores and the supplying manufacturers. Thus, if the Louisville Wal-Mart store sells two boxes of a brand of disposable diapers manufactured by Procter & Gamble, that sale will register with P&G in Cincinnati, and it will be P&G's responsibility to make sure that the Louisville store is restocked. Thus, the stores are never "temporarily out" of anything.

Naturally, this requires a great deal of flexibility on the part of the supplying companies to change from the old ways of meeting supply and demand, but by the same token, their products will not sell if they are not on the shelves of the stores. It's a win-win situation in the long run.

"The reason dinosaurs became extinct was because they would not adapt to changing environments," says Dr. Leonard. "The same will hold true of companies that refuse to change. Continuous adaptability is the key to economic survival."

And can this, you may wonder, impact entire industries? Most definitely, yes! Consider this: In the span of one decade (1981–1991), literally dozens of major and minor airlines went bankrupt because they refused to change over to supersonic transports, wide-bodied airplanes, frequent flyer bonus programs, and other customer-driven innovations. Among those filing bankruptcy were Allegheny, Eastern, Ozark, Pan Am, Braniff, Western, Frontier, Republic, PSA, Piedmont, and Texas International. The obvious lesson here was "adapt or die."

SECOND WAVE:
PASSIVE CUSTOMERS WILL BECOME MORE INTERACTIVE

Previously, customers waited to see what retailers would offer for sale. Then they would decide whether or not to make a purchase.

In the future, however, customers will want to be personally involved in the organizing, designing, and distributing of goods and services. Already there are significant evidences of the customer telling the retailer how and when and where to provide a service. One such example is in the marketing of college courses.

"In the past, most colleges would create a course, list it in a catalog, and then expect students to enroll in the class and come to the campus to attend the teacher's lectures," says Prof. James Roznowski, head of the math department at Delta College in Michigan. "That's changing, however."

Prof. Roznowski explains, "Today, it's not uncommon for several working adults in a downtown office building to get together a class of twenty-five people who need a certain course toward a bachelor's or master's degree. These folks will come to a nearby college and say that it is not convenient for them to attend class during nights or weekends. Instead, they would like to attend class during their lunch hour at their own work site.

"The college then must decide whether to meet this need by sending a professor to that location several days each week or to pass up the chance to enroll twenty-five new students. Naturally, colleges *never* want to pass on a chance to enroll students, so the registrar goes to work to try to make this class possible."

Several innovative options have been developed, reports James Roznowski.

"In one instance, the college asked the employers of these adult students to help defray the extra cost of bringing a teacher to the workplace, since regular tuition did not cover travel time or mileage for the professor. The employers saw the benefit of having their employees become better educated, so they provided the supplemental funds, as well as classroom space and furniture and educational equipment.

"In another situation, the professor stayed on campus, but presented her class lectures by way of televised transmissions. She would lecture in front of a camera; her students would watch her on monitors in their classroom some thirty-five miles away. The students would also have a camera available to them, and the teacher had a TV monitor. In this way, the students could ask questions and receive immediate answers.

"The point, however, is not *how* the need was met, but rather that it was the customers (students) who told the retailer (the college) what service was needed and how it had to be delivered. Customers are no longer passive bystanders. They now see themselves as the ones calling the shots."

Prof. Roznowski is right. In fact, with CD-ROM training, some students don't see the need for teachers at all. This means that when students do opt to pay for a college class, they are going to want "added value." They will expect extraordinary presentations, since what is being presented is supposed to be better than what they could learn on their own. This, in turn, will demand more interactivity on the part of the professor so as to determine how he or she can meet the *specific* (not generic) needs of the students.

Consumers of all sorts—not just college students—are going to become more vocal about what they consider "added value" to be. They will want more choices. They will insist on more advice and help in buying from suppliers. This will mean that retailers will need to have statistical data, multiuse options, and detailed manufacturing information readily available when clients come to "kick tires."

Double-Sided Benefits

But if it seems that the benefits of interactivity are all weighted on the side of the consumer, consider the many ways in which retailing companies and large corporations can also benefit.

"Teleconferencing and videoconferencing are going to save millions of dollars in staff development fees during the coming years," insists David DeHayes, president of the DeHayes Group, a Fort Wayne consulting firm.

"Consider how much it now costs small firms to send a person off to Chicago to attend a three-day seminar," says DeHayes. "The hotel bill ($900), the cost of the seminar ($1,200), the airline tickets ($350), meals and tips and taxi fare ($200), and the lost productivity by not being at work ($750) will make the event cost the employer $3,350. That's really hard to justify when trying to plan an annual budget.

"However," he continues, "look at what is saved when the seminar directors interact directly with the attendees by putting on the seminar via teleconferencing. The employer can bring a dozen employees into a room for one day, and all can attend the seminar via satellite without leaving town. For a flat fee of, say, one-thousand dollars, the employer gets twelve times the benefit for one-third of the cost. It saves time and money, while also expanding the number of people who can receive the information."

Some larger companies are taking interactivity to the point of creating their own private television networks that both provide information for employees *and* allow employees to respond with customized programming of their own. At Chrysler Corporation, for example, television monitors are positioned in factory lunch rooms, reception areas, corporate board rooms, and training areas. Chrysler has its own network that broadcasts industry news, stock reports about the company, information about its various products and new lines of cars, and feedback from trade shows, customer surveys, and dealerships.

"This network programming is beamed via satellite into each one of our facilities," explains Judith Griffie, director of training at Chrysler's world headquarters in Auburn Hills, Michigan. "However, each plant also has a small television studio that is used by the workers themselves. They do live or videotaped programs of news strictly of interest to that particular facility. They make birthday and anniversary and birth and death announcements related to the employees. They televise presentations of awards for customer service or quality control to workers in their plant. And they present sales and quota data for that one factory. It's totally interactive. An employee can watch Chrysler news or *be* Chrysler news."

Lean and Mean

One of the realizations retailers are going to have to come to in dealing with customers who want to be interactive is that businesses will no longer be able to be all things to all people. Instead, each business will have to do what it does best and shed the rest. If we entered the age of specialization during the twentieth century, we will take it to extremes in the twenty-first century. People will be quick to demand exactly what they want. The era of the passive customer is rapidly coming to an end.

THIRD WAVE: SHIFTING FROM HUMAN POWER TO AUTOMATION

In the late 1960s, when eight-by-four-by-two-inch handheld calculators came on the market, people began to throw away their slide rules. At that time, Texas Instruments had an early lead in this market. For approximately $128, plus the cost of four batteries, a person could buy a handheld calculator that could add, subtract, multiply, and divide. My, my, this was considered a phenomenal breakthrough in engineering.

Just a dozen years later, however, in 1980, the handheld calculator had been replaced by the "pocket calculator." It was the size of an average business card; it could add, subtract, multiply, divide, do square roots, run decimals, figure percentages, and had a memory bank built into it; and, as far as cost was concerned . . . well, if you would renew your subscription to any major magazine, you'd get one *free* as a little signing bonus.

This only serves to demonstrate how rapidly automation is improving. Progress in this area is exceeding science fiction. The communicator used by Mr. Spock in the 1960s TV series *Star Trek* was supposed to be a modern convenience of the year 2090—yet, in 1994, actor Leonard Nimoy, who portrayed Spock, had his photo taken with a cellular phone that was smaller, less expensive, and more powerful than the unit Spock had used in the "distant future."

Robots used in factories in 1996 are 50 percent cheaper than robots of a similar order made in 1988, yet they are 425 percent more efficient. Again, as costs decrease and efficiency increases, science fiction cannot keep pace with reality. In the 1990 motion picture *Total Recall*, Arnold Schwarzenegger is living in the year 2075. In one scene he gets into a taxi that is self-driven: It has a robot at the wheel and a computerized guidance system. In reality, Ford Motor Company has already developed prototypes of self-driven vehicles.

The question that quickly comes to mind is, "If we won't need taxi drivers anymore in the future, doesn't that imply that computers and robots will be doing many other jobs now handled by human beings? And, if so, isn't this a curse rather than a blessing?"

"It's a mixed blessing," admits John J. Harrison, syndicated financial columnist and author of *It's a New Day for Consumers* (Summit Books, 1993). "There's no doubt that as software continues to improve, automation will maintain its progressive course. The good side of that is that humans will be needed to construct the automation and design the software. The negative side is that machines are usually better workers than humans—they don't go on strike, they don't need coffee breaks or lunch hours, they don't call in sick, they don't ask for a weekly paycheck, the amount they cost the company is a tax write-off, and the work done by the machine is usually faster and more accurate than work done by humans. As such, employers are eager to find new and better machines that will allow them to downsize and replace their human workforce."

Harrison points out that even white collar workers are not beyond the invasion of automation.

"The New York Stock Exchange is currently installing a system to provide automated stock trading and underwriting services directly to people wanting to purchase stocks. Company reports will be available on-line, as well as all other research data about the companies. Buyers can skip the stockbrokers and make direct purchases, thus avoiding commission fees. There will be no need for brokers anymore.

"Similarly, there are many accounting and book-keeping programs already on the market which are making such clerical workers as accountants, tax consultants, and bookkeepers obsolete. People can just type in the numbers on their home computers, the software programs do all the figuring, and the word processors print out the bottom-line data. CPAs aren't needed for these procedures."

Harrison notes that even the most esteemed professionals, such as lawyers and physicians and ministers, are not beyond reach.

"There are computer programs that show people how to draft their own wills and business contracts," says Harrison. "Experiments are now being conducted to develop computerized robots that can use lasers to reshape the cornea so as to eliminate the need for eyeglasses. Thus, bye-bye to optometrists and even some ophthalmologists. Furthermore, the Bible is now on computer discs. Users can get the Hebrew or Greek original texts next to as many as six different English translations on the same screen. The program also has an index that references all words, names, locales, dates, and historical events found in both the Old and New Testaments. Who needs ministers when they can have all this data at their ready command?"

Counterpointing his own examples, Harrison says, "Naturally, there are human elements of these professions that machines cannot do, nor would we want them to. I wouldn't want a computer or a robot to preach a funeral or conduct a marriage ceremony or counsel me when I was having spiritual or marital or other personal problems. Still ... if interviews and global 'discussions' can take place on the Internet, who is to say that a sermon couldn't be sent by E-mail each Sunday to parishioners who don't want to get up early, get dressed in a nice outfit, and then drive all the way across town to attend a church service? It sure makes one pause to think, doesn't it?"

Listening to such predictions, historians will argue that such threats have been made at other junctions of history—the beginning of the Industrial Revolution, the onset of the Space Age—yet the vast majority of the population has always managed to find work. Futurists, however, consider this to be a comparison of apples to oranges. What happened in the previous ages, with their lower populations and slower technological developments, has no relation to the high-tech, supersonic, multibillion populated world of the twenty-first century.

Emotionally, there is a burden to bear. As children, we cried when the steam locomotive and the power saw beat legendary Paul Bunyan and his faithful companion, Babe the Blue Ox, in an all-day lumberjacking contest. It scared us to think that machines could outperform humans. Later, as adults, we were scared even worse when we watched Stanley Kubrick's screen adaptation of Arthur C. Clarke's *2001: A Space Odyssey*, and we saw the computer HAL decide on its own that the crew of the spaceship must be killed and that Dave, the ship's commander, must be ignored. HAL considered his data bank to be wiser than Dave's mere human brain. Thus, not only were the machines now outworking the humans, they were also outthinking them.

But did we humans pull the plug?

No.

Instead, when it came to developing new technology, we took a page from the Olympics: "Faster . . . Higher . . . Braver!" We created, and still are creating, machines that were and are more incredible than the generation before them.

And, good or bad, right or wrong, these machines

are going to remain a shaping force in the economics of the next millennium.

FOURTH WAVE:
FROM COMPETITION TO COOPERATION

It has been said that politics makes for strange bed-fellows. Well, of late, so does economics. Joint ventures, licensing agreements, technology advances, and corporate acquisitions are increasing on a daily basis. Cross-border alliances have tripled since 1990.

Sometimes it is a situation of old rivals seeing the value of group sharing, as when Ford and General Motors and Chrysler consolidated into one crash experiment site (not three) where they now share research data. (Hey, if Russia and the United States can work together in space, anything is possible.) Other times, it is a situation of former rivals finding it vital to unite forces in order to repel an even greater force, as when IBM and Apple and Motorola combined research efforts to develop the PowerPC chip in order to battle Intel.

There are many justifications for these new "co-ops."

First, they allow companies to tap complementary niches. The Little Caesar's pizza chain has started opening restaurants inside of K-Mart stores. It's a boon to both businesses. Little Caesar's benefits by selling food both to the customers of K-Mart *and* to the store's employees (a double market). K-Mart benefits because when people come inside to buy pizza, they often will make some impulse purchases at K-Mart. Additionally, customers are likely to stay longer at their shopping if they can take a quick break, buy a snack at Little Caesar's, and then go back to their browsing of the aisles.

The Subway sandwich shop chain has built some

of its new restaurants on the side of gas stations. Again, it's a double blessing: If people pull in for a snack, they'll probably also fill their gas tank; if they pull in for gasoline while on a trip, they can also get a quick take-out sandwich and a soft drink. Both businesses benefit.

Second, it allows businesses to share their areas of expertise. A good example of this is seminars held on cruise ships. The seminar directors show the cruise lines how to attract customers during the off-season ("Give people a cruise that is a tax write-off because it is the setting for a business seminar"), and the cruise lines show the seminar directors how to attract bigger crowds ("Offer them education in the morning, but visits to tropical islands in the afternoon, all at one flat price").

Third, it allows small and midsized businesses to enter foreign markets. If another business is already established in Europe, it makes sense for smaller businesses to try to become partners of that larger operation. They may have to share some of their profits, but if their overall income rises dramatically because of the new influx of customers, who cares? It will be well worth it.

Fourth, it creates funds for otherwise prohibitive ventures. As mentioned earlier, neither Apple nor IBM nor Motorola had the capital, time, or personnel to go head-to-head against Intel alone. Together, however, they were able to accomplish the mission.

Calling For a New Attitude

Needless to say, it is alien for most employees of one company to think along the lines of cooperating with their major competitors. Most people still harbor a "robber baron" mind-set in which you underprice your competitors until they go bankrupt or else you outperform them so that you steal away all their customers. However, the economic base has shifted, and so must the thinking of retailers.

In the 1950s, people did business with their local neighborhood businesses. In the 1960s, with the onset of shopping malls, consumers were willing to drive a ways in order to do regional shopping. In the 1970s, with mass mailings of catalogs, shoppers began to shop nationally. Today, with on-line services, they are shopping globally. To compete in such aggressive markets, businesses are going to need all the allies they can get . . . even when those allies are former adversaries.

So, a new attitude will be needed. For employees to interact with their new competitor/partners, they will need to show mutual respect and trust, a sort of "Golden Rule" style of management. There will need to be open lines of communication in order to diffuse any flare-ups or misunderstandings before such incidents drive a wedge between the new partners. Workers on both sides of the agreement will need to be treated fairly, equally, and respectfully.

Leadership in these allied companies will have to be highly involved in each co-op venture. Managers will have to remind employees constantly that the goal supersedes all turf battles or corporate cultural infractions. This won't come easily, nor will it come quickly. It will take time to cultivate such relationships. Nevertheless, if employees are looking for a way to hang onto their jobs, one of the ways this will be accomplished will be by beating business swords into plowshares, and planting and harvesting together.

FIFTH WAVE:
SHIFTING FROM MASS MARKETING
TO MICROMARKETING

For more than two centuries, America has been called the world's great "melting pot." That has never been the truth, nor will it ever be. There is no such thing as a "generic American," and, thus, there can never be a generic customer. In the future, this will become more and more obvious.

If America were a melting pot, then people from all the various cultures, ethnic groups, religions, social strata, and races would soon look, sound, and act identically after arriving in America. Nothing could be further from the truth.

For a fact, most Americans relish their personal heritages, and they refuse to suppress these legacies. The American of Polish background still likes to dance the polka and the czardas and likes to eat kielbasa and golombki. The American of Hispanic background enjoys Spanish guitar music and likes to eat tacos, enchiladas and burritos. The American of African background often prefers to wear braided hair and to use an African first name. And so it goes in different but equally valid expressions for Americans of Chinese, German, British, Russian, or any other nationality or cultural background.

Rather than a melting pot, America is a patchwork quilt. Each group is distinctive in its makeup, yet each group is interlaced with the groups surrounding it. Together, they form a multicolored, multilayered unit that "covers" the nation. Each one is as American as the next one, yet each has a distinctive personal identity. They even learn from each other. If this were not so, Taco Bell would not have become a successful food chain, Alex Haley's *Roots* and Amy Tan's *The Joy Luck Club* would not have been blockbuster novels, *Empire of the Sun* and *The Last Emperor* would not have been successful movies, Chef Boyardee and La Choy products would not now be standard grocery-store items, and Jean Claude VanDamme and Arnold Schwarzenegger wouldn't be popular screen stars.

So, the groups coexist, yet each has its own set of needs and perspectives, demands and desires. How keenly manufacturers target these needs will determine the difference between great and marginal success in coming years.

Some companies are setting the pace in this area by creating a niche within a niche. For example, during the 1950s, if a person wanted to purchase a soft drink, he or she would simply ask for "a Coke" or "a Pepsi" or "a 7UP" or whatever the basic soft drink product was.

Today, the Coca-Cola Bottling Company offers Coke Classic, New Coke, Coke II, Diet Coke, Cherry Coke, Diet Cherry Coke, Caffeine-Free Coke, and Caffeine-Free Diet Coke. Similarly, the Pepsi-Cola Corporation offers Pepsi, Lemon Pepsi, Crystal Pepsi, Diet Pepsi, Caffeine-Free Pepsi, and Caffeine-Free Diet Pepsi.

It used to be that you could send a kid to the store to buy a box of Tide. Now, you have to specify whether you want regular Tide, Liquid Tide, or Fragrance-Free Tide. If you wish to purchase a Delta faucet, you have to choose among plastic, brass, and stainless steel. And let's not even get started on the subject of the computerized fitting of specialty blue jeans.

These companies have recognized that different people like different things, have different needs. The companies have responded by developing "splinter" products to meet those needs. They have either modified their existing products or created new companion products. It has proven to be very successful for them.

But what if a company does not have the financial power or research and development resources of a Coca-Cola or Levi-Strauss conglomerate? For them, sometimes the answer is to prove that bigger is not always better.

There is a variety of ways of doing this. One option is to provide a less expensive, small-scale alternative product. For example, the line of colognes called "Imitators" has fragrances that are similar to English Leather, Old Spice, British Sterling, Jade East, and Chaps, yet at lower prices than those major brand names. Likewise, several small computer companies like to refer to their products as "IBM clones" that can interface with IBM software yet do not cost as much as an IBM computer, or keyboard, screen, and printer.

Some of these companies, because of their small-scale, well-run operations, can tap into emerging trends faster than larger, more bureaucratic companies. Some also are able to provide something that is not available elsewhere. Certain of these latter companies have been formed when larger companies did not find it cost-efficient to continue a certain line of goods because the market demand wasn't massive enough; nevertheless, smaller companies were delighted to work on these smaller scales. They controlled the entire available markets for those products. Their attitude was "I'll take my sliver of the pie. It isn't huge, but I will have all of it to myself."

Successful micromarketers also excel at spotting trends. They look diligently for markets overlooked by others. They do this by seeking constant customer feedback. As one retailer explained to someone he was surveying about his business, "I don't care how minor or insignificant it may seem. Tell me *exactly* what you want. The next time you contact us, we'll have it for you."

The days of the generic product for the generic customer are over. From now on, customization and personalization are going to be the key selling points of all products and services.

SIXTH WAVE:
MOVING FROM WHAT'S IN VOGUE
TO WHAT'S OF VALUE

As we noted earlier, Generation X will not have the earning potential that previous generations had. Nevertheless, consumers of today and tomorrow are not seeking cheaper products, just better values.

Now, what do we mean by "value"? Defining it in its simplest explanation, value is what a person receives (products or services) in exchange for what he or she is willing to give up (money, time, or convenience). For example, if a homeowner feels that $250 per summer is a proper fee for someone to charge for fertilizing a lawn, the homeowner will give up that much *money* in order to receive that service. If, however, the homeowner feels that such a cost is too high, the homeowner will give up some of his or her *time* and will go out and buy the fertilizer and will spend various days during the summer doing the work personally.

Of late, many businesses are discovering that today's customers are rebelling against annual price increases, premium-label market dominance, and high-profit markups. These customers are using clever strategies to beat the retailers at their own game.

"We buy in bulk," explains LuAnn Darnell of Phoenix, Arizona. "Several of the young couples in our neighborhood go in with us and we buy soap, cereal, canned goods, and household products by the case or truckload. With that much volume, we can get wholesale prices most of the time. It saves us twenty-five to forty percent of what we'd have to pay at the local grocery stores for the same items."

Another tactic is to maximize coupons. Cindy Sherrill, wife of a minister and mother of four sons in Churubusco, Indiana, says, "I have more than thirty shopping bags in my basement in which I collect box tops, proof-of-purchase seals, coupons, soup labels, and subscription offers. As soon as a bargain or offer comes on the market, I send away for it. I shop where stores offer double rebates on manufacturer's coupons. I subscribe to a coupon newsletter and learn of bargains around the country that I can cash in on by mail. I also swap, trade, and barter coupons with other housewives. For a few hours of snipping with scissors while watching television at night, I save my family thousands of dollars annually and gain us a lot of bonus items we might not normally be able to own."

Shopping in "prior-owned product" shops is also becoming popular. "Unlike boys, who can rent a tuxedo for one night and then give it back, girls need to buy their formal dresses," explains Pamela Rice Hahn of St. Mary's, Ohio. "When my daughter wanted a gown for her prom, we discovered that there were several shops in area towns that sold formals that had been used only once for a prom or wedding by the previous owner. They were still as good as new, yet at a third of the original cost. With a little bit of seamstress work, we were able to save a lot of money."

There are now prior-owned shops for everything from sports equipment to tools, from clothes to books. In the future, the demand for such used-but-still-good products will see many more such stores opening.

A Spoiled Clientele

If Generation X has less cash today to spend on items, that does not mean it does not remember "the good life" of living at home with Mom and Dad. The X-ers still want the same lifestyle they had when they were being reared by indulgent parents. This often causes them to demand more than they should have a right to expect; yet, if even one retailer yields to these demands, it creates a new level of expectation.

One arena in which this has been visible is the fast-food business. Traditionally, all fast-food restaurants prepared their hamburgers in a standard way. The customer came in, put money on the counter, and walked away with a sack of generic hamburgers. Then Burger King said, "Have it your way." Customers were told they could "hold the pickle, hold the lettuce" because "special orders don't upset us." So, people came in to try it out and discovered it was true: They could have a burger with no onions and no ketchup . . . or with *only* onions and ketchup. The generic hamburger had now been customized to meet exact customer specifications.

You can see where this led. If a customer who is used to getting his or her hamburger personally customized at Burger King then goes into Hardee's the following week and asks for a burger with no mustard and no pickles and is told, "I'm sorry, but all of our hamburgers are made up ahead of time in a set way," the customer will say, "Oh, then just cancel the order. I'll go down to Burger King where I can get it exactly the way I want it for no extra charge." This, in turn, forces Hardee's to offer "the works bar," where customers can add anything they want—and as much of it as they want—to the basic hamburger they have just purchased at the counter. And, naturally, Arby's, McDonald's, and every other hamburger chain quickly falls in line. The customers get spoiled very quickly. Customer "satisfaction" is determined by what the customers now expect and at what level those expectations are met or exceeded.

This battle of one-upsmanship can become a looping spiral that is about as easy to escape from as a tornado funnel. First, for example, Kentucky Fried Chicken offers fast-food chicken; then Famous Recipe offers fast-food chicken that comes in the "regular" recipe or in "extra crispy"; then KFC offers regular recipe, extra cripsy or "rotisserie style" chicken . . . and the battle continues ad infinitum. Retailers become their own worst enemies.

So, then, is there any middle ground? Can the retailers provide both the price values *and* the service excesses demanded by a spoiled generation of customers? The answer is yes, but only if the retailers are willing to make great efforts at developing creative tactics for coping with these new demands.

One tactic is to develop private-label goods that are equal to but less expensive than products with famous brand names. For example, in the sundries departments of many supermarkets, customers can purchase over-the-counter allergy medications, aspirins, cold capsules, toothpaste, mouthwash, and shampoo that carry the store's name. These items are about 20 percent less expensive than the nationally advertised brands, yet when the customer turns the packages over and reads the ingredients, the products are virtually identical. The customer gets the same high-level product he or she is expecting, but at a more reasonable cost.

Another tactic is to invest in labor-saving systems. At Service Merchandise, customers wait on themselves by browsing through the merchandise and then filling out a purchase form and bringing it to a central ordering counter. Their payments are accepted, and their products are then ordered and are brought to them at the counter. Thus, customers have access to all of the products they are looking for, yet they receive them at lower prices because the store does not have to hire floor clerks, department managers, or shelf stockers.

A third tactic is for retailers to consolidate suppliers. Instead of offering one basic product packaged by nine different suppliers all fighting for shelf space, stores are now saying that they will only carry two or three brand names. This means that where nine different companies used to be competing in one aisle, only three will be there now. But the three who survive the cut will be able to place greater numbers of each of their products and more varieties of their products on those available shelves. In exchange for this exclusivity, the retailers will insist on greater wholesale discounts so that they can, in turn, lower the retail prices to their customers.

A fourth tactic is for retailers to buy in greater bulk. Just as consumers have started to save money by buying in bulk, so have retailers. Retailers have found that by placing a huge order with a supplier at the beginning of a year, rather than ordering month by month, the supplier can provide a better discount to the retailer. The same products are purchased at a lower price, and the savings are passed on to the customers.

SURVIVAL STRATEGIES

As people continue to move rapidly from vogue to value, retailers will have to simplify their operations; the tactics of empire building won't work in the year 2000 and beyond. Retailers will have to help customers get "back to basics" in a way that will be cost-effective, yet will still be acceptable and pleasing to a spoiled clientele. They will have to develop a strategy of "value pricing" that will provide customers with options of services they wish to receive, yet still allow the retailer to survive. And, most importantly, they will need to capitalize on the concept of "added value," by knowing what the customers want and then throwing in a little something extra atop all that.

These, then, are the six waves of our economic future. Some are just now rising on the distant horizon, —whereas others are already right upon us. It's time to start paddling because the surf is definitely up!

5: Art, Music, and Literature After the "New Age"

FROM "BABY Boomers" to "Baby Busters" to "Generation X" to "the Millennials," society has made advances, retreated, surged forward, ebbed, regrouped, revised and revisited trends of every concept and variety.

In fashion, the wide tie was in, then out, then in again. The miniskirt has gone to the back of the wardrobe closet for short times but has never really disappeared. The butch haircut for men in the 1950s gave way to shoulder-length hair in the 1960s, then styled hair in the 1970s, and then back to closely cropped hair again in the 1980s and 1990s. Forays into body-piercing, dying hair green and spiking it, tattooing, and wearing underwear as an outer garment have lured a very small segment of society for usually a short time and have only served to underscore the fact that standard fashions are more cyclical than we tend to believe.

Similarly, politics has its cycles: FDR's four consecutive victories and Truman's follow-up victory made it look as though the Democrats would be in the White House forever. However, Ike spent two terms there; and subsequent terms by Nixon, Ford, two landslides by Ronald Reagan, and the follow-up victory of George Bush showed the Republicans were yet very strong. The legacy of John F. Kennedy, the solo term of Jimmy Carter (who came out of nowhere to win the White House), and the two-term elections of Bill Clinton (helped, considerably, by the third-party spoilage of Ross Perot) showed the Democrats were yet viable and aggressive. Politics has continued to run in cycles.

However, if fashion, politics, theories of education, military doves and hawks, and economic policies all do seem to create repetitive cycles, such is not always the case with art, music and literature.

The marriage of art and technology has created pixels that "paint" pictures on computer screens and then print them out with such high-resolution density, the machine-created art seems to excel above the works of artists using brushes. This is *not* the recycling of any art form that has previously existed.

The "pitch bend feature" of a recording studio wah-wah patch now enables sound engineers to reroute a singer's flat or sharp notes through a bend feature that can correct any errors of pitch, modulation, vibrato, or volume. In essence, the recording becomes a creation of a singer's best efforts—as "adjusted" by technology to elevate those efforts to perfection. This results in the finest compact discs, audiocassettes, and records ever made; yet, it manufactures recorded performances that can never be equalled in a live concert. This is *not* the recycling of any form of vocal performance that has previously existed.

Children's stories are being written on the Internet by having a narrator begin the story and allow herself to be interrupted constantly by World Wide Web contributors who want to embellish the characters in the story, add a subplot, offer new passages of description, or introduce a line or two of comedy. This is *not* the recycling of a system of creative writing that has existed before.

So it is, then, that art, music, and literature truly do seem to be breaking new ground in preparation for the new millennium. The artistic pathfinders are, even now, cutting trails that lead in that direction. Nevertheless, certain observers feel that without the core knowledge—the knowledge obtained from traditional training in the arts—no foundation will exist for these "breakthroughs." To that end, in this chapter we will hear from artists, writers, reporters, musicians, and teachers who will not only reveal the new expressions currently under development but also evaluate their merit.

THE FUTURE OF FILM

Dr. Wes Gehring, professor of journalism at Ball State University and the author of five biographies of famous actors and six books on the history of motion pictures, feels that some of the best work in film is being done right now. In an exclusive interview for this book, he shared his views on filmmaking.

Critics feel that the "golden age" of comedy filmmaking was back during the era of silent films. Do you agree with this?

GEHRING: James Agee's watershed essay in *Life* magazine (1949), called "Comedy's Greatest Era," has come to be the rock on which the silent movies stand. Until recently, I had endorsed it wholeheartedly (and it is still book that no one can touch Chaplin). But I now lean more toward the nineteen thirties. There's the delightful screwball comedy genre of *The Awful Truth* [1937] and *Bringing Up Baby* [1938]. Add to that the nineteen thirties works of the Marx Brothers, Laurel and Hardy, Mae West, Will Rogers and W. C. Fields, plus the fact that Chaplin was still filming during this era, and you've got an amazing array of comedic talent.

Having said that, I must admit that the silent movie era did produce two master artists who have never been equalled. Buster Keaton and Charlie Chaplin wrote their own movies, directed them, and were the leading actors in them, and Chaplin even composed the play-along music for use in the theaters by the organ or piano players. That's incredible! Admittedly, Fields did write his movies and star in them, but he did not direct. Of course, there is a wonderful irony in that, too, when one considers that W. C. Fields and the Marx Brothers were *impossible* to direct, so there was always a certain negative control being exhibited by them over their directors."

Trick photography created a great bar drinking scene with Bob Hope in Son of Paleface. *[1952]. In 1996, computer graphics were used to create the wild scenes with Eddie Murphy in* The Nutty Professor. *Are these gimmicks cop-outs for screen comics who cannot match the physical comedy of Chaplin, Keaton, and Lloyd?*

GEHRING: Yes and no. True "thrill comedy" has to have the comic and the danger in the same film frame, such as Chaplin and the lion in *The Circus* [1928]. Without that, there's a sense of cop-out. Yet, special effects have always been around, starting with Melies at the turn of the century. Even the film pioneers, such as Keaton, were fascinated by camera tricks, as evidenced in scenes in his *Sherlock, Jr.* [1924]. We now know that even Harold Lloyd used a stunt double at times in *Safety Last* [1923]. Besides, we still have some great contemporary visual comics. Steve Martin did a brilliant job of walking, talking, and sitting as if half of his body was male and half was female in *All of Me* [1984], and Jim Carey did jumps, flops, rolls, dives, twists and turns in *Liar, Liar* [1997]. These actors can stand with the best of the silent-era performers.

With the development of CD-ROM graphics, why are people still going back to watch W. C. Fields, the Marx Brothers, and others in grainy black and white?

GEHRING: For one simple reason: You cannot watch those films without bursting out with laughter. Beyond that, placed in their slot in time, they are masterpieces of filmmaking. People entering the extreme next millennium—the year three thousand—will still be watching these old films and still enjoying them.

Comedic actors such as Eddie Murphy, Robin Williams, and Richard Pryor have brought off-color language to the movies. Will audiences of the future expect more of this or begin to reject it?

GEHRING: Four-letter words have been around since the closing scene in *Gone with the Wind* [1939], and they are here to stay in movies. Such language is the norm with a performer such as Richard Pryor. Other times, it is used just for one scene, such as the f***ing car-rental scene in *Planes, Trains and Automobiles* [1987] with John Candy and Steve Martin, which otherwise would have been a PG-rated movie. Certain critics have said of Richard Pryor that his blue language represents a "theater of the real." Even *New Yorker* critic Pauline Kael has likened Pryor and his shtick to a contemporary Charlie Chaplin, had Chaplin been able to speak.

In June of 1996, Disney Studios announced it would make fewer feature films each year from then on. Does America have too much movie entertainment to choose from?

GEHRING: It isn't just from film. America has too much overall entertainment to choose from. Nevertheless, I don't expect the Disney decision to set a trend. For that matter, during the studio era in Hollywood [1929–1946], the film companies made many more films, including short subjects and so-called "B" films, than are being made now. Besides, even bad films can turn a profit today by going quickly to video.

How will home entertainment centers of the future impact theaters?

GEHRING: When video stores were just starting to open, many people questioned the future of theaters. But video popularity has just fed the popularity of theatrical screenings. Tomorrow's home entertainment center should have the same effect. Video rentals allow a viewer to become more of a student of the film. He or she will see films ordinarily missed, and this only increases that person's interest in more movies, perhaps based on a given director or performer or genre.

Why did people stop going to drive-in movies after 1975?

GEHRING: You won't see a revival of the old drive-ins in the next millennium. Drive-ins served primarily as a place for young people to be alone for necking and making out. The movies were usually double-feature, low-quality films (because nobody was watching). During the 1970s, dating rituals changed. Parents were absent a great deal of the time, so young people had privacy at their own homes. They also had air conditioning and no mosquitoes. This eliminated the need for drive-ins.

How has the VCR changed Hollywood?

GEHRING: The VCR is the greatest thing that ever happened to Hollywood. It has provided vast new sources of income for Hollywood via video rights and cable rights. Many low-budget movies are released directly to video. It's a new outlet for what once was considered the "B" movie. Today, films can fail at their big-screen opening, only to be discovered later on tape. Sometimes this has meant a new big-screen release, both here and abroad. Regardless, people involved with the production are receiving all the important recognition.

Controversial and/or huge critical film successes can find several lives on video, too. For example, *Dances with Wolves* [1990] scored twice on tape: first as a small-screen release and later as the "director's cut" with added footage that had not originally appeared in the movie. Hit movies going to video can sometimes offer a special incentive for purchasing them, such as the interviews with the director and stars of the movie *The Player* [1992], which were added to the end of the video release of that movie."

Has anything disappointed you about the movie business?

GEHRING: I did not approve of the colorization Ted Turner did of so many of the great black-and-white movie classics.

Robert Redford's Sundance Film Festival is trying to encourage small, independent filmmakers. Will we see more of this in the future?

GEHRING: Trying to make a living in movies is always a big gamble, but the more the movie festivals encourage small films, the greater the opportunities that will arise for the independent filmmakers. Personally, I feel an even greater chance for small guys is in the specialized cable market.

If you were to make a prediction of the films made since 1985 that people will still be watching well into the next millennium, which ones would you choose?

GEHRING: In no priority order, I believe those films would be *Schindler's List* [1993], *Pulp Fiction* [1994], *A Fish Called Wanda* [1988], *Pretty Woman* [1990], and *Fried Green Tomatoes* [1991].

What screenwriters, directors, or producers do you think will be the power forces in the year 2000 and beyond?

GEHRING: Most of them are already working today—Steven Spielberg, Oliver Stone, George Lucas. Quentin Tarantino should be projected as a power of the future, but his body of work is still rather small despite the success of *Pulp Fiction*. If I had a surprise name, it would probably be Ron Howard. He has an impressive film list already, and he's relatively young. And I think Rob Reiner might be knocking on the door, too.

Also responding to questions about the present and future status of film was award-winning writer, director, and producer Bill Myers. Myers received a degree in stage directing from the University of Washington and a degree in filmmaking at the Italian State Institute of Cinema in Rome. His more than forty awards include three New York International Film Festival honors, nine ITA Platinum Video Awards, and fourteen Silver Angel Awards. His 1996 documentary *A Cry for Freedom* received eighteen thousand high-school booking requests within the first three months of its release. Myers, who has also written thirty-six books, makes his home in California.

"I insist on staying active in both the printed medium and the visual medium," says Bill Myers. "With one hundred channels on cable TV and 8-quad movie theaters, our modern audiences are overdosed on visual media. I read recently that a person today who is twenty-five years old and has only read six books is in a lot of company. That's scary. The greatest theater of all is the human imagination."

He continues, "The quality of films is contributing to this problem. As more and more studio films become nothing but bigger and bigger carnival rides with little artistic, thematic, or intellectual substance and no insight into people and characters, I think there will be a new hunger for more thoughtful films in the next century. In the past year, I've had continued contact from independent producers wanting to talk to me about two-to-seven-million-dollar projects. These are very small budgets in the scheme of modern-day filmmaking; nevertheless, the scripts for these projects were moving, gripping and thought-provoking."

When asked which big-budget filmmakers he feels

will be around for years to come, Myers echoes Gehring in his choice of Oliver Stone.

"I don't think anybody comes close to Oliver Stone as a director," says Myers. "I don't always agree with Stone's world view, but nobody can use the medium the way he does. With his release of *Nixon* [1995], he has proven that, besides all his superb technique and storytelling tools, he can also get deep into a character. Stone is a genius.

"I'm big on character development in film. I was trained in Europe and began my career as an actor. As a writer and director, I had to learn how to make plot just as important as characters in order to hold the attention of American audiences. My work always has strong themes because I have strong beliefs, and if I can successfully marry all three elements of character, plot, and theme, the piece works."

Myers's 1990 movie *Bamboo in Winter* was filmed on location in Asia and told a story of modern Chinese trying to sort through ideological battles between politics and religion, heritage and progress, family and community. He cites it as a "piece that worked."

When asked if he were twenty-two today and wanted to get into filmmaking, what he would do, Myers responds, "I would make every effort to get directly involved in any aspects of the production of movies—as my day job. At nights, however, I would study writing and I'd work at writing. Very few people in film work really understand writing and the art of storytelling. There are notable exceptions, such as Oliver Stone and Francis Ford Coppola, and to some degree Penny Marshall and Billy Bob Thornton. They use their craft to tell a story rather than try to wow an audience. I'm not crazy about some of the new directors because they either don't understand the rules of good narrative or they simply break the rules so as to be known as a rule breaker. I believe that the best directing is the directing that moves an audience and tells a story without drawing attention to the directing."

When asked about the use of the new television rating systems, Myers says he is in favor of them. "I think," he explains, "that the rating systems are good starting points for helping families discern the impact that a show will have on viewers, especially the way HBO also states the various reasons for the rating. But the taboos of sex, violence, and profanity are only half the concern. Before my own two children see a film, I make just as sure that I am aware of the theme or world view it is promoting."

For the experts like Gehring and Myers, filmmaking seems to be borrowing the best from the past, in that modern performers such as Steve Martin and Jim Carrey can benefit from the slapstick antics of Buster Keaton and Charlie Chaplin; but in regard to such innovations as video rentals, independent filmmaking, and cable-television direct film sales, Hollywood is headed in directions that are all new and primed with potential.

LET'S MAKE MUSIC

James Riordan has spent his professional life reporting on the music and film industries. Among his numerous books are *The Platinum Rainbow: How to Succeed in the Music Business without Selling Your Soul* (Swordsman Press, 1980); *Making It in the New Music Business* (Writer's Digest Books, 1987), *Break On Through: The Life and Times of Jim Morrison* (William Morrow & Company, 1991); and *Oliver Stone: The Controversies, Excesses and Exploits of a Radical Filmmaker* (Hyperion, 1995). For seven years, he wrote a nationally syndicated column on music while also freelancing for such periodicals as *Rolling Stone* and *Downbeat*.

"One of the first things I am usually asked," says Riordan, "is why music always seems to be evolving into new areas, yet the older types of music are not replaced. Well, to begin with, that isn't a correct assumption. Certain records and styles of music are a lot like certain dances which become all the rage for a season but then are never heard from again (the Freddie, the fly, the stroll, the Bristol stomp, the Watusi, even the twist).

"What makes it 'seem' as though certain forms of music have never gone away is a subculture interest, such as the fact that Peter, Paul, and Mary can still draw a good crowd to a concert despite the fact that folk singing died out after the sixties, or because one medium will stimulate an interest in another, as when a movie such as *Dirty Dancing* or *Scent of a Woman* will create a craze to learn how to tango or waltz and, thus, bring back the big-band sound for a time."

Riordan continues, "However, there are other examples of music styles that show no sign of disappearing or waning in popularity. One such example is the pop/rock sound of the nineteen fifty-five to nineteen seventy-five era, encompassing the early rockabilly sounds of Elvis and Bill Haley, the British invasion of the Beatles and Stones, the Motown sound of Smokey Robinson and the Supremes, and the jukebox kings and queens ranging from the Four Seasons to Brenda Lee. Across the United States, there are 'oldies' stations that play these tunes continually, and they are listened to by folks from ten to seventy-five. The recording quality may be better today than ever, but people have never purchased recordings because of recording quality (and particularly not young people). There's something about the music of the pop/ rock era that withstands the test of time. The tunes have a strong pop feel with a message. I call it commerciality with heart. That's a hard combination to beat."

But how did the decade *after* "pop feel with a message" present its music? Riordan claims it was without the message.

"Maybe the message became too heavy toward the end," speculates Riordan with a shrug. "With Hendrix, Joplin, Morrison, and so many others who made millions but killed themselves with booze and drugs, dropping like flies, the public opted for a neutral period. The message became passé after the heavyweight rock prophets of the sixties and seventies. Disco was safe because it said nothing. Eventually, however, people grew tired of lyrical pablum. Rap was born then, a medium that stressed the lyrics. That, too, was soon overdone; so, now, as we head toward the year two thousand, people are looking for deep meaning in a well-written, solidly musical song."

When asked to ponder what changes are ahead for music as an industry, Riordan says, "The visual will become equal in importance to the audio. MTV has made that a reality. Already, performers have to look good and move well and come off well in a video *in addition* to having a hit recording. In a true sense, MTV is the number one radio station in the world, in that it showcases more hit records and new artists than any other medium.

"Similarly, onstage performances have become an art form unto themselves because today every pop performer has to find a way to become larger than life. I'm convinced this trend will continue for as long as technology gives performers new and better ways to outdo each other—giant balloons, flying wires, massive screens, huge sets."

But what of the social conscience of recording artists, Riordan is asked.

"Kids like to be shocked, and it's natural for teens to want to rebel," explains Riordan. "Rap music milked that tendency to the max, but when it began to chant such messages as 'Kill a cop,' it failed to draw a line between what is wrong with society and what is wrong with mankind. That's dangerous, because in the late nineteen nineties, kids started looking for truth—even spiritual truth—in their music. Artists such as Live, Seal, Tori Amos, Collective Soul, Joan

Osbourne, Alanis Morissette, and others ask spiritual questions—something that previously had always been frowned on in pop music. But the questions are so honest and the answers so needed, the kids are responding."

Riordan supports his premise by offering facts about the religious music element in contemporary airplay.

"Young people buy more recordings than anyone, so record companies monitor their desires closely," explains Riordan. "In nineteen ninety-one, it shocked record producers when a little company called Sparrow Records sold a million copies of *The Champion* by Christian vocalist Carmen. They wanted a piece of this growing market, so by nineteen ninety-five such mainstream companies as RCA, Liberty and Fore-Front had introduced new lines labeled 'Contemporary Christian' music."

According to *Forbes* (January 2, 1995, p. 40), seven Christian music albums were certified gold or platinum in 1994. Chain stores, including Best Buy and Blockbuster Music, started offering entire sections of Contemporary Christian recordings. In March 1996, the Christian rap group D. C. Talk released "Jesus Freak," which had sales of 85,841 copies the first five days on the market. Within days, a "Jesus Freak" video was on MTV's light rotation. By early 1997, mainstream radio stations were playing recordings by Michael W. Smith, Jars of Clay, Point of Grace, and Amy Grant, all best known for their recordings of Contemporary Christian songs.

"Let's be realistic about this," cautions Riordan. "The recording companies and radio stations and TV networks aren't offering this material because they have some kind of ministry objectives. They're in it for the money. Nevertheless, the fact that religious recording artists are now producing material with arrangements, lyrics, and sound quality of equal sophistication to secular artists, combined with the fact that teens and older listeners are eagerly buying these recordings, proves there is a solid market. Ask me the reason, and I'll say that the nihilism, the off-color lyrics, the violent themes, the lewd references to women, and the raucous sound effects of secular music are leaving a lot of young people cold. If any trend is unfolding for the future of music, it's this: Young people want up-tempo music, but they also want meaningful lyrics."

But what of the composers, lyricists, singers, and instrumentalists who don't get connected with the major recording labels or music-video production companies? Will there be any place for them in the future? According to James Riordan, the opportunities will be greater than ever.

"There is a company in San Mateo, California, called Headspace, Incorporated, whose CEO is a man named Thomas Robertson," reports Riordan, "and his company's entire mission is to upgrade Internet sound quality to the point of allowing new artists a chance to present their material on the World Wide Web by totally skipping the recording companies. Once this becomes reality, virtually anyone can find an audience for his or her songs."

At present, Robertson's company is paying its way by making Web sites more musical, but according to *The Wall Street Journal* (March 20, 1997, p. R-17), "Headspace is creating a music and sound component for Sony Corp.'s WebTV, which delivers Internet service through television sets. But Headspace's biggest development so far is a soon-to-be-released Web-based software system, Beatnik . . . which will enable Web sites to play music constantly, a soundtrack that can be altered or influenced by the user."

James Riordan explains, "So, what we are seeing with companies such as Headspace is the ability for a performer to record music, distribute it over the Internet, and even transfer it eventually to home television sets. Now, if they can just figure out a way to guarantee royalties for all that, some people are going to get very rich during the next millennium."

COMPUTERS AS ARTISTS

Nowhere is the battle between traditionalists and revisionists being fought more fiercely than in the field of graphic arts. It's pixels versus paintbrushes, and high-resolution printers versus hand-brushed canvasses. Conservative artists are arguing that high-tech graphics are not really art at all, but merely computer programs formulating a series of lines and colors. More progressive artists say that, rather than replacing traditional art, computers are opening the doors to creativity for those artists brave enough to explore their potential.

"Technology has always had a major impact on art," says critic Sarah Miretti. "When metal paint tubes were invented in the eighteen hundreds, artists were free to move out of their studios and into nature. When the camera was invented, it gave artists a way to 'freeze' the scene before them. It also left them free to explore interpretation, rather than simply capture moments in time.

"Now, the computer is generating an artistic revolution even bigger than these inventions," continues Miretti. "Combining portability with potential, computer programs provide new freedoms—not only from the studios, but also from the limitations of traditional paint and paper. As some analysts have expressed it, what the machine did for freeing the body, the computer is doing for the brain."

Miretti asserts that talent will never be replaced by a microchip; however, she feels the techno-artists of the future will be better equipped to explore their own types of art by pulling together the best of old and new.

"It will be an interactive creativity," explains Miretti. "The modern artist will have a database of artistic lessons and examples to call up and study, even to emulate, although in a more contemporary setting and with better and brighter colors and greater capacities for depth perception and vibrancy. Who is to say that works by Matisse or Picasso or Rembrandt wouldn't be even more compelling in three-D or as holograms? We'll soon be finding out."

THE PRINTED WORD

During the 1960s, the BeeGees sang a song with a refrain that explained, "They're only words, but words are all I have." Although it was meant to be a love song, it could have been the theme song of publishers, editors, journalists, novelists, poets, lyricists, and advertising executives. These people have one bag of tricks: the dictionary. They live or die by the power they have to use words.

"Outside of the human brain," Dr. Elton Trueblood, author of thirty-four books, once proclaimed, "there is no such thing as a word processor. Machines can sort words, type words, spell words, categorize words, and define words, but they cannot process a sequencing of words that will hold readers spellbound. Only writers—talented, educated, disciplined writers—can do that."

One individual who has dedicated his professional life to the study and sale of words is Thomas Clark, editor of *Writer's Digest* magazine. A former newspaperman and college writing instructor, Clark also has kept busy as a freelance writer, with bylines in everything from sports magazines to *Modern Bride*. Recently, he served as project editor for the book *Making Money Freelance Writing* (Writer's Digest Books, 1997). Clark travels the nation as a guest speaker at writers' workshops and conferences, offering his insights on the future of the printed word. He shared several of these insights in an interview he granted specifically for this book.

Are hard copy newspapers and magazines on the way out?

CLARK: My gut instinct is that it won't happen in my lifetime (and I've just turned forty). CDs, electronic mail, the Internet, and all things wired and electronic are not passing fads, certainly, but they'll likely never match the portability of paper. Oh, sure, I can punch up a freshly updated text of the daily newspaper online, and soon I'll be able to see it displayed on my television set (which will be connected to the Internet as well as cable); but, until someone designs a laptop I can prop up against the sugar bowl and that won't fry its circuits when my five-year-old spills OJ on it, that online version of the newspaper can't do what my paper version can. And, yes, I could print out the text to take to the table with me, but who wants to? For me—and most other people—to accept a new technological advance, it must do a task better than what I've already got and more conveniently than I can now do it. Rarely will the public accept an improvement that accomplishes only half that equation. The same thing goes for magazines and books. Until someone makes a computer that can be read comfortably at the beach, I don't envision people abandoning paper publications.

Is writing becoming techno-dependent?

CLARK: No. Software is simply a tool to help the human brain work better. Spell checkers can't tell the difference between to, too, and two, and even if the day comes when they'll be able to, the computer won't know if we mean "Do you, too?" or "Do you also?" or "Do you two?" (as in, "Do the two of you?"). Only the writer's brain will know.

The same goes for grammar checkers and style checkers: They may balk at a forty-word sentence, but where would F. Scott Fitzgerald or William Faulkner have been without those sentences? Good writers won't surrender such judgment calls to a computer. And if they try, readers will stop reading them because they won't find in their text the surprises of great writing.

And as for writing-aid software, it doesn't do anything but prompt you to dig deeper into your own mind. No software could have told Margaret Mitchell, "Have Rhett tell Scarlett he doesn't give a damn," much less have told Mitchell to phrase it more memorably as "Frankly, my dear, . . ." It could have challenged Mitchell: "Is your conclusion memorable?" and "Is your dialogue crisp?" and even "Make the characters' last exchange short; put it in one sentence." But "Frankly, my dear, I don't give a damn" is a writer at work, and no computer can or will ever replace that.

As for software that can supposedly "duplicate" another writer's style: So what? Why would I want to read computer-generated Fitzgerald (much less Jacqueline Susann) when I can read the real stuff? And if the day ever comes that a computer writes an "original" work, it will still be the programmer who wrote the software. To write, you must think and feel and comprehend. Computers respond to input. Big difference. And from that difference comes writing.

Do Web pages help or hurt writers?

CLARK: Both. They help in that they make it possible for more people to see a writer's work. They also make distribution of work easier, and even make it possible for writers to sidestep editors completely. With little investment, a person can launch her own on-line "magazine" and promote it pretty darn well, too. She can decide which of her stories people will see. Collecting money for that work is a problem at present, but technology will catch up on that pretty soon. In terms of getting work *out there*, the Web is great.

Of course, that's part of the downside, too. Once it's *out there*, it's easy for the work to be copied and retransmitted to places the writer didn't want it to go. And all too often (with even *once* being too often), the writer's byline doesn't make the journey with the rest of the text. So, it's easy for the writer to lose control of her work.

Also, some publishers seem to believe that because they published a work in the hard-copy magazine, they have the right to publish it on-line without additional payment to the writer. Sorry, but no! Even the most sophisticated on-line operation isn't a simple reproduction of the magazine. It's a new product, and writers deserve to be compensated for their work's use in that *new* publication.

You still make time to teach college courses in writing. Are you teaching students today differently from the way you were taught?

CLARK: As far as techniques of writing and editing, no; my lessons are still the traditional lessons of grammar, syntax, punctuation, transitions, spelling, style, and format, combined with insights on research, reporting, interviewing, meeting deadlines, and maintaining professional ethics. However, in the area of technology, I explain to my students that they must become familiar with word processors and computers. I emphasize that just as the typewriter replaced the pen, the computer has replaced the typewriter. I explain that editors of the very near future are going to want to have virtually everything sent to them electronically. For many publishing ventures, that aspect of the future is already here.

You have been an editor for twenty years. What do you like about it, dislike about it, expect will change about it?

CLARK: The most enjoyable part of my job is getting to play with words all day. Face it: This isn't digging ditches or hauling rocks. My head may ache from bad writing, my ears may ache from overly long phone calls, my eyes may be red from reading copy, and my fingers and wrists may go limp from too much typing, but this will never be manual labor. Nor is it brain surgery. If I screw up a story, it's almost certain that no one is going to die. And, on a good day, I get to help people learn something, or do something better, or simply enjoy their lives more completely—if only because they simply enjoyed the half hour, day, or week they spent reading my magazine.

The least enjoyable part of my job is rejecting the works of writers, telling them that the words they've put so much effort into "don't meet our current editorial needs." I don't like to inflict pain, even if it is just part of the writing business. I don't lose sleep over it very often, and I have even been known to take a bit of delight in rejecting the material of some overly self-important souls, but the rejecting is the biggest downside to the job. That and not always having the resources to do all the things I want to do with the magazine. But in that latter complaint, I'm not different from editors throughout time, including those yet to arise in the future."

The Right Kind of Writing

If Thomas Clark is an apt representative of editors' perspectives on the future of the printed word, then Peter Jacobi is equally able to comment on that topic from writers' perspectives.

Author, columnist, and college journalism professor Peter Jacobi writes regularly for the *The New York Times, Saturday Review, Chicago Times* and even *Highlights for Children.* As a reporter and historian, he has written sections of the *World Book* and its annual *World Book Yearbook.* His textbooks include *The Magazine Article: How to Think It, Plan It, Write It* and *Writing With Style: The News Story and the Feature.*

"There has never been a more exciting time than now and the near future to be a writer," says Jacobi. "I tell young people that the world is their 'beat,' and the world is their competition. With technology the way it is, it is easier to access data than ever before; however, it is also easier for everyone else to access the same information. It's a race!"

Does this mean that he feels writing itself has changed greatly? No, quite the contrary.

"Recently, I read the closing scene of *The Trojan Women* [416 B.C.] to some of my students," explains Jacobi. "Euripides wrote that scene some twenty-four hundred years ago. It's a speech given by a grandmother as she laments the needless death of her little grandson, a sidelines victim of a long and bitter war. The words are so powerful, hearing them makes you want to cry. When I finished that speech, I paused a moment, then picked up a copy of *Time* magazine and read an account of a thirteen-year-old black youth named Delphonic McCray who was shot to death because he happened to cross into a housing project area controlled by a certain gang. The writer of the article let the boy's grandmother tell about her great loss, of how she had just bought the boy his first real suit and how, now, it would be used for his casket and burial. The story was pathetically sad, and its parallel to the Euripides speech was not lost on my students. Since themes of human tragedy do not change, the need to express them powerfully in words also does not change."

Jacobi does admit that the current and future times are leading to new topics to write about.

"When Dolly the sheep was cloned in Scotland in early March of 1997, people immediately began to ask if it would soon be possible for humans to clone themselves and multiply that way," he notes. "Yet, two weeks later, the Heaven's Gate mass suicide took place in California, and people began to ask if humans were mastering ways to eradicate themselves systematically. As shocking as both stories may have been, they were marvelous counterpoints to each other and proved that we are living in amazing times. Each day is a new journalistic adventure." Jacobi refers to writers as travel agents and travel guides because they not only use their words to take readers to all the places of the world, but also to the past and future.

He says, "In Thornton Wilder's play *Our Town*, Emily comes back from the dead for one day and proclaims, 'Oh, earth, you are too wonderful for anybody to realize. Do any human beings ever realize life while they live it, every, every minute?' As journalists, I feel that is the level we *must* live it.

"I don't ask my students to like to write. I surely don't. What I do ask is that, once they take up the task, they become compulsive about it. I tell them to know that they *have* to do it, and not for a grade or a job, but to enrich the life of somebody else. That is their opportunity, their possibility as journalists.

"I encourage writers to write about things that will make readers want to question things, not leave them puzzling over what the writer was trying to say. Thus, writing must be organized and clear and succinct. However, writing is an art, not a science, despite formulas of approach and structure that have to be drummed into the beginning writer by necessity. Writing is an art because it is done by a person who is a creature of experiences and traditions, who, nevertheless, is acting in spontaneity. The writer puts down words in response to people met, places experienced, and events witnessed. Writing is voice with style, done with a grace and ease that suggest that the writing must be done exactly this way, as though formed that way in nature. No attention is drawn to the writer, just to the writing's message and images. This calls for blood, sweat, and tears on the part of the writer, but that struggle must never be evident in the finished product."

Carrying ahead with his theme of writers as travel guides, Jacobi says that writers are mapmakers of their own worlds. A writer's words, though only ink on paper or typing on a screen, are symbols of adventure, pleasure, challenge, and discovery.

"Without writing, there would be no idea to instigate, no move to activate, no direction to navigate, no compulsion to investigate, and no likelihood to participate. But writing requires courage, especially when family, friends, and critics are looking on. To write, one must brave the rapids of life; and as journalists, we do, not just because it is our job, but because we know lives can be changed."

Jacobi asserts that the greatest challenge for writers in the next millennium will be the same greatest challenge writers have always faced—i.e., to know their audience, their readers.

"Let me explain it with a story," he offers. "A missionary was sent to a poverty-stricken village of Peru. He invited the village's farmers and animal tenders to hear his first sermon, in which he explained to them what heaven was. He used abstract touches of philosophy but saw only expressions of puzzlement on the faces of those listening to him. So, he picked up the Bible and read from the book of Revelation. This baffled his listeners all the more. He stood there frustrated and feeling like a failure, until suddenly a thought occurred to him. He cleared his throat, looked at the crowd, and started his sermon all over again. 'Heaven,' he told the people, 'is like a village with no mosquitoes.' Instantly, he had the rapt attention of every person. He had figured out, at last, how to communicate with his audience. In the future, the challenge will be similar, whether trying to communicate with Yuppies or Millennials: Writers will have to speak their language and will need to focus on topics that will intrigue."

When asked if he can offer some guidelines by which writers of the future can succeed, Peter Jacobi offers his Ten Commandments for Writers:

1. Be sensitive to your audience.
2. Be confident in your belief of your subject's merit.
3. Be specific, and offer concrete information.
4. Be yourself by remembering the *U* in y-o-u.
5. Be perceptive, and glean meaning from the issues you cover.
6. Be clear.

7. Be liked, not as a person but as a writer.
8. Be courageous by breaking the chains of predictability.
9. Be passionate so that the readers know you care.
10. Be ready to listen to both what is around you and what is within you.

"Writers of the future should not be content with what they have done before or with what other writers have done before," asserts Jacobi. "They should be experimenters, iconoclasts, who break away from the predictable with language, with attitude, with approach, and with perspective. Therein lies the excitement."

Web Magazines: Where Old Meets New

While writers and editors both will espouse the virtues of traditional writing styles and modern word-processing capabilities, some editors have begun to anticipate the needs of the next millennium by creating periodicals that reflect the reading needs of the times. Even though Thomas Clark said he could not envision a morning newspaper on a laptop that could not be leaned against his sugar bowl, other editors have already begun to create such periodicals.

"Each day, new magazines are being created for the World Wide Web," explains Pamela Rice Hahn, a computer-age communications specialist whose articles have appeared in *Atari Explorer*, *Current Notes*, and *S T Log*. "True, some of them disappear just as fast as they appeared, but at least forty are gaining a wide readership. Among these are Microsoft Corporation's *Slate*, which covers current events and personality profiles; a creative-writing magazine called *Dream Forge*, which features interviews with working writers as well as works by poets and authors; *Salon Magazine*, which focuses on trends, heavy-metal music, small-budget films, fashion, and food; and *Feed*

Magazine, which explores contemporary issues at a deeper level than the mainstream press is delving into."

Hahn is a full-time freelance writer and critic. She says that since the start of 1997, more than 75 percent of her writing assignments have been for on-line magazines.

"It's a wide-open opportunity for freelancers because these Web magazines have such small staffs," Hahn explains. "Usually the entire operation is run by two or three editors who dole out assignments to freelancers. The magazines support themselves through visual ads, much the same way a free E-mail service such as Juno does. Some of these magazines attract as many as twenty-five thousand readers each week."

Hahn points out that there are substantial differences between hard-copy magazines and on-line magazines.

"Readers are content to subscribe to a hard-copy magazine that comes out once each month," says Hahn. "Readers of on-line magazines see screen magazines as something akin to television. As such, they 'reopen' the Web magazines expecting to see new material on a daily basis. Very few of the magazines are able to meet such demands."

Hahn also points out that a hard-copy magazine can be purchased by libraries as a historical record that can be used as a research document in the future. However, Web magazines that try to evolve and change frequently provide no such capability.

"The problem of charging for subscriptions to these magazines is the biggest challenge," says Hahn. "Drawing twenty-five thousand readers each week to your Web magazine does not mean you are making any money from this. Still, there are magazines that don't necessarily need to show a profit. For example, an in-house newsletter or magazine for a trade union or a veterans' organization or even a religious denomination could find funding from its parent operation and go on-line merely as a service to its membership. That's just one way these new Web magazines might end up 'paying' their way."

OVERVIEW

One message all critics seem to share in regard to the future is that technology will never replace the originality of the creative artist. Whether that artist works in paints, lyrics, film, or the printed word, the distinctiveness of thought that comes from the human mind will not soon (if ever) be equalled by machines. The machines, however, will enable the artist to explore his or her imaginings to greater heights.

Perhaps that will one day be recognized as an art form itself.

6: Sports in the Era of Virtual Reality

DURING THE next ten to fifteen years, technology will become so advanced, U.S. golfers will be able to play a round of eighteen holes at St. Andrew's in Scotland without having to cross the ocean . . . tennis matches will take place with opponents lining up to serve on courts thousands of miles apart from each other . . . and contemporary professional teams will be able to compete against the lineups of history's greatest players.

All this may seem impossible to you when you consider the distance of both space and time. How can a person in America be playing golf in Scotland? How can a team in the year 2009 be competing against the 1929 New York Yankees or the 1962 Montreal Canadiens or the 1967 Green Bay Packers? The answer can be given in just two words: virtual reality.

Already on the market are games known as simulators, which are the stepping stones to what one day will be genuine virtual reality (VR) games. The simulators use graphics to imitate sports action events and motions, but an actual VR unit will make the participant feel as though a real game is taking place and he or she is part of it.

Genuine VR has distinctions that today's simulators can't come close to re-creating. True VR has a headset for each participant. Inside the headset are two separate video lenses, one for each eye. The lenses are set at precise angles so as to blend the vision of both eyes across one accurate viewpoint. This produces the best possible re-creation of depth perception and visual imagery.

Another advantage true VR has over simulators is the ability the players have in regard to freedom of movement. Most simulators limit participants to one location, in that they stand or sit in front of a stationary screen; from there, the viewers interact with the video image projected on the screen.

VR, however, is much more realistic. With a headset in place, a player looks not just to the front, but also to the sides, behind, below, and above. Simulators cannot match this sort of realism. In VR, the player is *in* the game—perhaps not physically, since his or her eyes are tricked into seeing only what the game wants the player to see; nevertheless, it's a full range of vision.

Sensors mounted on the headset monitor the slightest turn or nod of the head. With each movement, the game reacts by showing the player what would be seen according to the direction being looked in from inside the game.

Another advantage that VR will have over simulators is the fact that tactile sensations will be part of the game; players will actually be able to feel the sun and wind at a tennis court, the grip of a golf club, the powdery dryness of a rosin bag or the twanging sensation of a released bowstring.

Some VR experiences will require the participant to wear a full body suit with controlled air-pressure pockets inside the suit. These air pockets will make the participant's fingers feel the size and weight of a baseball or basketball by applying air pressure to the fingertips. Although no piece of real sports equipment will exist, it will seem as if it does as long as the participant keeps the headgear on (in order to "see" the imaginary ball) and wears the air-pressure suit (so as to "feel" the imaginary ball).

VR has also begun to experiment with adding fragrances, odors, and aromas to the headgear so that during a baseball game, the player would smell everything from the popcorn in the grandstands to the new-mown grass in the infield.

Putting It To Use At Home

But how will all this high-tech VR make its impact on the average sports fan? Let's suppose a businessman arrives home from the office and decides he wants to have a couple of hours of fun before he has to go out for an evening meeting. He might decide to take a little batting practice in a VR batting cage.

At the game's opening menu, he could choose from endless different environments—a sunny day in 1901 at newly constructed Fenway Park in Boston or a windy evening in 1989 at Candlestick Park in San Francisco. He will also be able to choose who he wants to throw batting practice to him: Cy Young, Roger Clemens, Denny McLain, Whitey Ford, Sandy Koufax, Don Drysdale, or Bob Feller. He will even be able to choose the temperature, the number of people sitting in the bleachers, the weight and style of the bat he'll use, and the number on his uniform. Sight, sound, smell, and touch will all be involved in this session in the VR batting cage.

Having keyed in all the information he wishes to encode at the options menu, he will then put on his VR helmet. Once it is on, he will "virtually" be at the ballpark, ready to take his cuts at the plate.

As he stands in the batter's box facing the mound, he will turn his head left and right to scan the scene before him. He will look down along the freshly marked baselines; he'll spot some fans moving down by the fence, hoping to snag an occasional foul ball; then he'll turn his attention to the mound, where the pitcher is dropping the rosin bag and getting ready to deliver the first pitch. From behind him there will be chatter from the catcher, and then the coach will shout, "Okay, let's see what this guy's got."

Play then begins. The pitcher winds and delivers. It's fast and inside, but the batter swings anyway. He connects with the ball, but it goes foul behind the third-base dugout. The next pitch is low, but it's in the strike zone. The pressure is on. The batter picks up on the fact that the pitcher is rotating the ball in his glove and spending time getting a special grip. This probably will be the curve. Sure enough, the ball comes in tight and then breaks, but the batter is expecting this. He times his swing, connects perfectly, and watches the ball sail deep into left field. Nice hit.

He continues to gauge sliders, pitchouts, breaking pitches, change-ups, and more fast balls and curves. Some get past him, but others he hits solidly, feeling the impact as bat and ball make contact. What a life, what an experience, what a—

"Honey! Hurry up and come in for dinner or you'll never make it to your meeting on time," interrupts his wife, calling from the kitchen.

Reluctantly, the player will realize it's time to remove the headgear and come back to the working world. Just before he does, however, he will no doubt take one last look at his surroundings—the stands and fans and vendors, the batboys and umpires and players, the mound and bases and home plate. Yes, he'll have to get back here again very soon.

And, with that, the headgear will come off, and the man will once again be standing in the middle of his basement.

Such a scenario is inevitable. Sixty years ago, sports fans would not have been able to predict the radical changes that were about to invade their beloved games—night baseball . . . domed stadiums with air-conditioning . . . instant replays . . . free agency . . . AstroTurf. . . .

VR will be the one radical change of the future that will impact both amateurs and professionals. A blending and overlapping of reality and VR will be the norm in the sporting world of the future. Consider, for example, the situation of the Portland Trailblazers of Oregon. The team plays in a $262 million sports arena called the Rose Garden. But team owner Paul Allen is already considering plans for constructing a VR entertainment complex next door to the Rose Garden. Marshall Glickman, team president of the Trailblazers, says, "My mission is to integrate Paul Allen's world of computers and communications with my own world of sports."

On the other side of the nation, in Washington, D.C., the Bullets and Capitals opened their new $175 million MCI sports complex in 1997. The arena will not only be home to Washington's NBA and NHL franchises, but it will also house a virtual reality sports center. Andrea Sarkisian, a member of MCI's public relations department, says that MCI is going to hold back details about the VR aspects of the center, except to say that it will be state-of-the-art.

Meanwhile, Jerry Jones, owner of the Dallas Cowboys, has plans during the next five years to build a theme park devoted to the theme of football. It, too, will include VR games, experiences, and training.

Jaron Lanier, the creator of VR, insists that most of the sports-related VR games are still on the drawing boards or in the imagination of someone's mind. Still, Lanier admits that significant advances have already been made.

"Greenleaf Medical Systems in Palo Alto, California, uses virtual reality in its physical therapy units," explains Lanier. "A virtual reality glove was used to help Joe Montana recover from a hand injury. He was able to practice his passing without ever having to pick up a real football."

Lanier, himself, did experiments in which he placed stereo cameras inside football helmets in order to create a more experiential form of sports spectatorship. He also had meetings with the Olympic Committee in which he suggested the development of a new form of baseball that would be played on a four-dimensional diamond and would allow the players to fly.

"I'm sure it will happen someday," says Lanier. "With as much money as Americans pour into the areas of entertainment (theme parks, movies, videos, games, toys) and sports, the financial backing is not a problem in developing these products."

It was Lanier who coined the term "virtual reality" in the year (how appropriate) 1984. According to computer guru Bill Gates, "Virtual reality will allow us to go places and do things we never would be able to do otherwise." In the development stages at present are video mapping, immersive systems, telepresence, mixed reality, and fish tank virtual reality.

Video mapping allows the user to watch a video of his or her real body as it interfaced with the virtual world it encountered in a game or travel sequence or training experience (see "BattleTech" explanation later in this chapter). An immersive system is an experience like the one described at the batting cage earlier in this chapter in which the participant enters completely into the virtual world. Most often, they employ head-mounted displays (HMD) that channel the sights and sounds received by the participant.

Telepresence links remote sensors in the real world with the operator, who is immersed in the virtual world. This system is being used by NASA as a way of helping astronauts learn how to feel "in touch" with everything on Earth while still floating in the soundless, odorless, weightless depths of outer space. The concept of mixed reality merges telepresence with VR by having computer-generated inputs blend with commands from real-world inputs to form the most logical procedures for navigation, space mapping, and landing projections.

Fish tank virtual reality combines a stereoscopic monitor display with a mechanical head tracker to create a virtual world.

"Play Ball" ... Sort of

Rather than speak of game experiences in theory, let's get first hand reports of three specific games and sports—BattleTech, bow hunting, and golf—as they were experienced by participants who engaged in state-of-the-art VR encounters.

Jonathan A. Yeh served as the on-site researcher for BattleTech. Yeh and some fellow journalists visited the BattleTech facility at Circle Center Mall in Indianapolis and filed this report:

"All pilots assigned to trainee mission Gamma 44 can now head for the departure area. This is your first call."

The message came blaring above the clatter of the other pilots moving about in the waiting room. It was 6:40 P.M. and time to start a new adventure.

The call sign given to me was "Hooney." We were now in the year 3051 and my mission was to translocate to the abandoned area on the desert planet of Solaris VII at 1900 hours and to destroy anything that came into the view of my rangefinder. (On a more personal note, I actually considered my mission to be just getting through my first VR experience without embarrassing myself.)

My friend "Havoc" and I had been checked in at the reservation area twenty-five minutes earlier by a crew chief everyone referred to as "Chaos." We carefully examined the briefing guide Chaos had given us and made mental notes that would help us survive our nine-minute inaugural mission.

"Why don't they just call me Danielle?" Havoc asked me as we stood together. She was as clueless about the VR game of BattleTech as I was.

"I don't think the name Danielle strikes as much terror into the hearts of our enemies as does Havoc," I answered. "Let's just go with it, okay?"

Reluctantly, she nodded. This was the first of three VR games we were scheduled to engage in that night on the fourth level of Circle Center Mall in Indianapolis. When I had told her I was taking her to Virtual World, I hadn't given many other details.

As we walked to the departure area, I felt as though I was ready. I had pored over the briefing guide, scanned other pilots' mission reviews on video, and I'd even sat in the cockpit simulator to familiarize myself with my new battle environment.

However, nothing could have prepared me for this. Certainly not the years of being Pac-Man champion at my area arcades, nor the numerous times I had played Tetris on the computer in the middle of math class in high school. Why, not even the hundreds of hours I had logged playing "NHL Hockey" and "John Madden Football" on Sega Genesis would provide an edge today. This was a whole new game. Literally.

The only thing I could do now was trust my instincts and pray that Ace, Shuggie, and Havoc, the other pilots, wouldn't blow me out of the desert.

Merchisio, another flight technician, checked our group in at the departure zone. He gave us a quick briefing on the controls we'd be using and the screens we would see in the cockpit. He was dressed in a bluish-gray lab coat, a nice cross between scientific and make-believe. He ran our names through the computer and told us we were set.

We next were led into the fenced-in containment bay where the battle would take place. It was dark, even dreary, with a yellow rotating police lamp providing the only light. We climbed into our egg-shaped cockpits and Merchisio clicked the doors shut. There would be no practice. When my cockpit lit up, it would be time for war.

I quickly surveyed the inside surroundings of my BattleMech (or "Mech," for short), the two-legged tank in which I was at the helm. My left hand controlled the throttle; the right hand controlled the joystick. My trigger finger fired all of my main weapons except for my missiles, which were launched by my thumb. It all seemed easy enough. Well, time would tell.

Since we were all trainee pilots on our first mission, we were fitted with Loki models, which were bigger, slower, and more heavily armored than other BattleTech models. At least the playing field was level.

But what about strategy? Would Danielle—er, Havoc—and I remain comrades, or would we betray each other and go our separate ways? It was an easy choice. I've always been rather independent.

Suddenly, amidst my reverie, the cockpit filled with light. I could now clearly see the sandy wasteland where the ensuing battle would take place. Reality or not, I was now at war.

It took me a few seconds to adjust to the controls. I assumed that everyone else was having some difficulty at first, too, since this was everyone's first experience with VR.

I began to use my radar to search for other targets. Aha—I found Havoc and began to target in on her. Just as I was about to thumb away a barrage of missiles, I felt the impact of direct fire against my left torso. It was only thirty-four seconds into battle, and already Ace had damaged me. I staggered, but kept Havoc in my sights and fired. Some of my missiles made contact with her body armor, but I inflicted no serious damage.

My heart was pounding. I could see the other Mechs moving in on me. I was a novice, so I fired wildly at anything that moved. Heck, the mission was to destroy anything that moved, so I kept firing. Unfortunately, I got hit more times than I hit.

Ace continued to fire at me, and soon a direct hit by him destroyed my upper right leg. This seriously limited my range of motion and momentum. My reverse throttle was rendered useless. I had no choice but to hobble forward in an effort to escape the beating I was taking. As I started to flee, I looked up to discover Havoc's Mech running straight at me, firing laser guns as she ran. I returned fire and tried to evade, but it was hopeless. She rammed me solidly, and on-screen I could see that we were both toppling to the ground.

I had actually jumped backward a few seconds before the collision, anticipating the impact (which, by the way, was seen but never felt). It all seemed so real.

Havoc disengaged herself from my Mech and went to do battle with the other two adversaries. I eventually managed to get back upright, but my left side was now paralyzed. I could see Shuggie in the distance, so I fired at him and blew a gun right out of his Mech's hand. This only served to draw his attention to me. He turned and launched a missile, and suddenly the entire inside of my cockpit was pitch black. All noises ceased. I had been destroyed.

Shortly thereafter, Merchisio's voice came over our intercoms, telling us the battle was over. We slid open our canopy doors and stepped out.

Ace and Shuggie began arguing about who had been the better combatant. Merchisio settled the debate by presenting everyone with a computerized scoring chart. It read as follows: Ace, 6,758; Havoc, 3,793; Shuggie, 2,459; Hooney (me) 2,362. Without a doubt, Ace had been far better than any of the rest of us, but it hurt my pride to have been bested by Havoc . . . Danielle.

We were led to a review room where our game was replayed for us on a VCR screen. As I analyzed my style of battle ("shoot at anything that moves"), I realized that panic was not a successful stategy for this game.

"It could be worse," Havoc whispered to me as we watched my Mech disintegrate on the screen.

"Oh?" I said. "How so?"

She smiled wryly. "It could be *real.*"

Lance C. Stiver did the research legwork for information on archery simulators. Not an archer himself, —Stiver nevertheless came away impressed by what high-tech was doing to bring Robin Hood into the twenty-first century. Here is Stiver's report:

For Bob Kacsor, archery simulators were invented at just the right time. "I really have a problem with hunting for sport," he says. "I hunt game only for the meat. I don't feel it is ethically right to hunt just for fun."

Kacsor was the winner of the 1996 Easton/Dart Indoor Safari, the largest archery contest in the world. This simulator archery contest was held in the spring at 151 sites throughout North America. The competition attracted 5,570 archers, who competed for the title and a top prize of three thousand dollars, according to Dart International's field operations manager Fred Eichler.

Kacsor had won several target competitions in the past, but winning the Easton/Dart Indoor Safari was an extra-special honor.

"The experience was very similar to hunting, except that you don't have to kill anything to win," says Kacsor. "That made it very enjoyable."

Being a resident of a small Indiana city, Kacsor experienced his first bout with archery simulators at the local archery shop. There, he found Gaylynn Sipe, manager of the shop, ready to get him acquainted with the new technology.

"We've only had the simulator since nineteen ninety-four," says Sipe. "It was a very new idea, and the hunters loved it. They have been able to stalk several different types of game, ranging from large animals such as elk, deer, bear, and turkey to such small animals as groundhogs and squirrels. During the winter, hunters usually need appointments because we stay that busy with the equipment."

The hunt takes place in a long, dark corridor. The simulation projection system places its images on a large Kevlar screen positioned at the end of the room. This type of durable material is needed to keep the arrows from piercing or damaging the screen.

The hunter stands approximately sixty feet from the

screen when firing. The arrows the hunter uses are specially tipped with a "blunt end." These special tips have a reflector which reflects the light projected on the screen as it hits. Instantly, the computer picks up the reflection and pinpoints the area of the screen the hunter has hit.

As the action begins, a sequence of "nature scenes" appears, each featuring a different animal. Hitting the animals in the scenes is extremely difficult.

"There is a certain time in each scene when the hunter has the optimum time for a kill shot," explains Sipe. "It must be clean and deadly. If, for example, the hunter shot through a bush in order to kill a deer, the points awarded for the shot would drop significantly even if the computer registered it as a kill shot."

Sipe continues, "The placement of the shot on the animal is the most crucial element. Bow hunting is different from hunting with a rifle or shotgun. With a gun, you aim and pull the trigger, and the animal is as good as dead because of shock. Bow hunting is more precise. Archers always aim for the heart or lungs. It's a matter of making the animal hemorrhage."

Bob Kacsor explains why this is so. "You have to hit the animal in just the right spot or else it can wander along for five or six miles without feeling a thing. It's like a razor-blade cut—you don't even know you have it until you see the bleeding."

When the simulation deer is in the open and positioned so that a precise shot to the lungs is possible, the hunter pulls back the bowstring and lets the arrow fly. *Thwapp!* If the arrow hits the screen directly in the shoulder area of the deer, a bull's eye appears around the area of impact, and the screen flashes "0 points awarded . . . Not a Kill Situation." That round has been lost, so the archer must try to do better in the next sequence.

The next time, a bear might be the target. If the hunter shoots the arrow and hits the image in a kill spot, the screen will flash "10 points awarded."

Gaylynn Sipe recalls, "We paid more than twenty thousand dollars to set up the simulation system, and then we leased the software from Dart International Incorporated. They allow us to upgrade our laser-disc sequences and scenarios at minimal costs."

Sipe feels the advantage of the simulator is that it gives hunters a chance to practice on moving targets rather than fixed bull's-eyes. Additionally, she believes it educates novice bow hunters as to where the kill zones are on various animals.

Bob Kacsor agrees. "The game not only lets you know where the kill zone is, it tells you immediately if you have hit it or not. This is the best possible training for the real thing."

Kacsor appreciates the way technology has made it possible for him to bow hunt without having to kill animals. Sipe is more pragmatic: She just appreciates all the business it brings to her shop.

Jonathan A. Yeh, zealous reporter from the BattleTech episode, filed the following report about indoor golf becoming par for the course:

It's a bone-chilling twenty-three degrees outside, and the wind is whipping the snow around in blinding swirls. Nevertheless, you decide to grab your clubs and play a quick eighteen holes of golf.

More and more people are finding a new way to enjoy the game these days: by playing it indoors. Thanks to golf simulators, everyone from PGA members to weekend duffers can enjoy a pleasant round of gold in a comfortable indoor climate.

Golf simulators, first introduced in the 1960s, are basically interactive video games. An image of a golf course is projected onto a large screen in front of the player, who sees the entire course as if he or she were playing at the links.

From there, the golfer steps back and hits the ball toward the screen. Approximately two million beams of infrared light per second pick up the ball and judge its speed, spin, direction, and angle. The simulator then projects the ball's image onto the screen, showing it flying toward the green (or perhaps into a sand trap or water hazard) just as it would at the country club.

The simulator then brings up the next screen, showing where the ball lies, and the golfer prepares to repeat the process. Golf simulators allow participants to play much faster than if they were on a real course since they don't have to walk or ride a cart two hundred yards between each shot. Even better, they don't have to wait ten minutes for the hack ahead of them who is going to take six strokes trying to get out of the sand trap. A foursome playing eighteen holes can finish a course like Pebble Beach in about three hours. These simulators are so advanced, a 486 PC model is now 98.3 percent accurate.

"The simulators provide every kind of shot, from hitting your tee shot on the back tees to putting out," reports L. J. Sweeney, the golf pro at Foster Golf Course in Fort Wayne, Indiana. Sweeney also supervises the golf simulators at "The Classroom" at Pierre's Entertainment Complex in Fort Wayne. "Virtually anything that can happen on a real golf course can also happen here. If you usually slice the ball outdoors, you're going to slice it on the simulator, too."

John Burton, a PGA member and the head pro at the Fort Wayne Country Club, agrees that the 486 simulator is very realistic, but he has found a few glitches in it.

"A simulator will never be one hundred percent accurate," says Burton. "They don't control pitch-and-run shots very well, and they sometimes allow golfers to hit a ball over trees that would be too high to clear on a real course. Still, they provide a good way to maintain practice when snow or wind or rain prohibit going out on the course."

In the northern and midwestern states, simulators at places like Pierre's are busy from 130 to 150 hours per week during the winter. Some businessmen come by for a "quick nine" during a long lunch hour. Other players enter simulator tournaments for two-man best ball contests, winter leagues, and even eleven-week eighteen-hole tournaments.

The people who benefit most from simulators, however, seem to be beginners. Novice golfers can take private lessons with an instructor on the simulators and never have to be embarrassed about how short or how off course a ball goes.

"The simulators are ideal because they allow you to work on the fundamentals of your swing," says Sweeney. "Beginning golfers can concentrate on their techniques without worrying about any of the outside elements found on a real golf course."

The simulators also feature a driving range where beginners or avid golfers can hone their skills. The simulator tracks the ball and provides feedback on the trajectory and speed of the ball.

"It's great for teaching principles," says Sweeney. "Golfers are able to fine-tune their swings using the information the simulator provides them."

Unfortunately for some golfers, the simulators are a little too realistic. Because of this, golfers have been known to shout the same sorts of expletives at the simulator after a bad shot that they are known to yell on the real course.

"One thing I haven't seen as yet on a simulator," says L. J. Sweeney with a chuckle, "is a vision of a putter flying into a tree after being thrown by a golfer who just missed a four-foot putt. But then again, that's an element of realism I don't mind foregoing."

THE DARK SIDE OF CYBER-REALITY

While all of the advantages of VR and simulation sports activities may be evident, there is also a dark underside to these "games" that researchers contend may present greater dangers than the offsetting benefits. Known by its nickname of "cybersickness," the phenomenon of no longer being able to distinguish virtual reality from genuine reality is a mental disorder scientists are still trying to understand.

Manufacturers of VR games and simulators often claim that cybersickness is nothing more than common motion sickness, such as that experienced by some people when going on carnival rides or flying in an airplane. Other people investigating the problem say it is much more serious, however.

Frank Biocca, a researcher at the University of North Carolina at Chapel Hill, reported that a female colleague of his was testing a VR headset designed for surgeons. After using it, the woman was so disoriented that, instead of taking a sip of soda pop from a can, she poured the drink into her eyes (*Technology Review*, July 1995, p. 14).

Similarly, Kay Stanney, a cybersickness researcher at Essex Corporation, reported that a young person who had spent an extended period of time playing a VR game lost his sense of depth perception and accidentally stabbed himself in the eye with a pool cue when he later took off the VR helmet.

Physicians explain that the reason people develop cybersickness is because there is a certain lag time before the computer image responds to the user's head and body movements. This causes a sensory conflict between what the individual sees and what he thinks he should be seeing. These delays confuse the brain and upset the inner ear's balance system.

The amount of time a person spends in cyberspace also complicates the problem. The longer the time, the greater the chance of experiencing cybersickness. Manufacturers of VR games know about this, and that is why they limit the time a person can spend in the virtual world.

But what will happen when VR games and simulators enter the homes? There will be no way to regulate how long children spend in the virtual world.

Accident-related incidents will surely increase.

Some VR companies tried to head off this problem by reducing the immersive nature of their games. They redesigned the games so that the players were involved partially in the real world and partially in the virtual world. This did, indeed, reduce the lag time responses from the brain and decreased the confusion; however, the players complained that the games were no longer any fun. What was the point of experimenting with VR, they said, if very little was virtual.

Corporate psychologist Robert Kennedy, who specializes in human-and-machine interactions at Essex Corporation, explains the VR challenge this way: "Virtual reality is what it says it is. It's absolutely compelling realism. That's its strength and its intrigue. To take away its ability to immerse a person in another world is to take away its allure. That's not to say, however, that it doesn't require elements of caution when being used."

In his experiments, Kennedy has seen people experience cybersickness in the form of flashbacks as late as six hours after using a VR unit. "When these episodes occur, they can be hazardous," says Kennedy. "One man involved in our studies had to pull his car over to the side of a road while driving home because he couldn't discern whether his steering wheel and dashboard and windshield were real or virtual. This was many hours after he had completed his VR experiments for that day."

Kennedy says that other researchers have reported cybersickness and flashbacks having occurred as late as an entire day after experimentation. The brain has continued to wrestle with the problem, even in daydreams and nightmares and everyday activities.

Ironically, research done by Kennedy and others seems to point in conflicting directions. On the one hand, the longer a person spends in cyberspace, the more apt that person will be to experience cybersickness. On the other hand, the only way currently known to overcome cybersickness is to spend a vast amount of time in cyberspace until the brain finally figures out how to compensate for both worlds—real and virtual.

"You can adapt to the discrepancies," says Kennedy. "It's not unlike the way astronauts get used to weightlessness or sailors get used to a rolling ship or tightrope walkers get used to heights. It's an odd feeling at the beginning, but with the passing of time, the brain can get adjusted to it. The main difference, however, is that sailors and tightrope walkers don't have flashbacks to when they were in their nontraditional environments. Victims of cybersickness do."

Kennedy believes that improved VR technology is not going to cure cybersickness. Because simulation is make-believe, there will always be a need to readapt to the real world when returning from VR. According to Kennedy, the cure to cybersickness lies in improved neuroscience, not in engineering.

"Some of the things that cause the problems are not fixable," claims Kennedy. "When you are perfectly adapted to the virtual world, can you simultaneously be adapted to the real world? That isn't logical."

So, until science develops some brain exercises for VR users that will reduce disorientation, VR games will have to be used with discretion and caution.

AND WHAT ABOUT THE MORALITY FACTOR?

In addition to the physical side effects caused by VR, some philosophers and members of the clergy are warning that VR may also cause emotional, psychological, spiritual, and sociological damage to individuals and society as a whole.

"Here is a challenge we members of the clergy are now being faced with," says Rev. Bill Herald, a sheriff's department chaplain and youth minister. "The bible teaches that whatsoever a person thinks on at great length, that is what will mold and shape that person's actions and behavior [Proverbs 23:7]. Well, if a person can simulate illegitimate sex, human torture, child molestation, or murder through the use of virtual reality, is that person blameless because these actions aren't actually taking place? My answer is no because, like Pavlov's dogs, these people are programming themselves to think this is acceptable behavior. The next step will be for them to attempt it in the real world."

Howard Snyder feels that many of the video games now on the market have already made young children insensitive to the pain and needs of others. By spending hours each week "realistically decapitating their foes in VR games that become an extension of their own hands, feet, and minds," this insensitivity can only increase ("The Cybergeneration," *Christianity Today*, Dec. 13, 1993). Snyder says parents are already seeing, in their children, antisocial behavior that reflects an emulation of the actions of video-game heroes. Kicking, hitting, stabbing, and shooting are part of the "game," and an entire generation of young people has now grown up finding it hard to distinguish between imagination and reality.

Prof. Don Hubin of Ohio State University's department of philosophy is not ready to concede that actions done in a world of virtual reality can be equated to actions in the real world. However, he sees validity in examining the situation.

"Look at the problem from a different perspective," suggests Prof. Hubin. "If a researcher develops a VR model of some phenomenon—a protein molecule, an aircraft, whatever—it's really easy to start relying more and more on the model than to do the actual hands-on research needed to confirm one's theses. The possibility of getting lost in the technology and forgetting to go to the real world for confirmation could exist. That could result in invalid research and, thus, dangerous consequences. It would not only be poor science, but also immoral behavior if the results were injurious to other people."

Though the idea of getting lost in the virtual world is frightening in itself, VR has set the stage for other ethical concerns as well. Hubin believes that the question of whether or not VR use is ethically wrong lies in deciding where its wrongness is located. Depending on "whether or not the wrongness exists in the intention of the person doing the action or in the effects of the actions themselves" will determine if VR is ethically right or wrong, Hubin explains.

For example, if a VR game allows someone to experience what it feels like to torture someone, is that game morally wrong?

"Suppose someone is playing that game," says Hubin. "Is that person acting immorally? He or she is not really hurting anyone, but is it wrong to engage in simulating torture? Some people think it is just as wrong as the real thing, whereas others consider it just a game."

The question, he reaffirms, lies in where the wrongness is located. "Is it wrong to seek the feelings of torturing someone, or is it wrong only to do it in real life?" asks Hubin. "You cannot deny that it is a concern of ethics, even if no one gets hurt." His point is that the wrongness is located in the intentions and aims of the user and not in the effects of the user's actions.

The more a person engages in violent actions in the virtual world, the more likely it is that this person may become less sensitive to human suffering. According to Hubin, the fact that VR has the ability to distort and trivialize important events in the real world should make it a serious concern for all people.

Certain promoters of the violent VR games and simulators take a more liberal view of the situation. According to them, in a virtual environment there are no consequences for immoral actions (no arrests, trials, fines, or imprisonments). And if there are no consequences, then nothing in VR can be considered immoral, and, therefore, it is a world in which anything and everything is permitted.

This, obviously, is in direct opposition to what is enforced in the real world. Prof. Hubin notes, "An immoral act in virtual reality is going to have a consequence on you and your character. To that end, I can understand why some people feel it's wrong to do it. These same concerns arose in the early 1950s when people debated about the good and bad aspects of television. Now, half a century later, we can see that some of those early concerns were exaggerated, but other concerns were right on the mark. Ultimately, the technology is amoral. It always comes down to whose hands it falls into and how it is used."

7: Technology—Servant or Master of Mankind?

OFTEN, THE very thing we take the most pride in regarding our advances in technology is simultaneously the thing we fear the most.

A prime example of this is found in military preparedness. According to military analyst George Friedman, author of *The Future of War* (Crown, 1997), the United States is developing a missile that can travel twenty times the speed of sound and can be targeted with such accuracy, it can be fired from a California desert and within ten minutes explode against a barracks or tank or convoy truck in North Korea.

"Whoever controls space also controls the battlefield," says Friedman. "The age of guns and bullets is over. The future will be an age of 'smart weapons' and precision-guided munitions. It now appears that the United States will be the leading nation in this area. Its space-based reconnaissance capability enables it to detect a threat and launch a high-speed missile before any harm can befall its people."

Friedman says that even advanced nations, such as Japan and Russia and China, lack the technological advancements and the financial backing to compete in this military arena with the United States. The twentieth century ground-based armies of these nations are no match for the twenty-first century capabilities of America.

"The United States, because of its space-age military power, will be the dominating force in the Americas, Europe, and Asia in the next millennium," says Friedman, who chairs a strategic forecasting committee. "The U.S. can influence economic and political events in both the Atlantic and the Pacific, something the Chinese, Japanese, and Europeans can't do. This puts the U.S. in a powerful position. The U.S. is the only world power that is both a continent in size and politically united. And it's sitting at the center of gravity."

Whereas all this technological advancement would seem to make the United States a safer place to live, there are critics who say such technology is the *real* enemy.

"Who are we kidding when we assume that just because we can create mass destruction at a farther range and at faster speeds than other nations, that this equals peace?" questions Dr. Ken Brown, director of the Peace Studies Program at Manchester College. "Has an escalating of war materials ever gone long without being matched or even superseded by one's enemies? The building of a more threatening weapon virtually compels one's adversaries to do the same."

So it is, then, that the face-off occurs. On the one hand, there are immediate benefits that come from advances in technology; on the other hand, those advances create their own reasons for anxiety, worry, and uneasiness.

Individuals have speculated over the years on how to deal with this dilemma. The classic science-fiction movie of the 1950s, *The Day the Earth Stood Still*, offered this solution: Build a population of preprogrammed robots (Klatu) that will kill anyone who tries to use technology in an illegal or violent way. Practical? Yes. Desirable? Goodness, no!

Others have suggested a "return to nature" program in which people should abandon all technology and retreat to the forests and live by chopping wood, trapping animals, and raising vegetables. Of course, there are flaws to this strategy, too, not the least of which is the fact that very little wilderness is left on the planet.

No, the fact remains that technology will continue to advance; so, it is up to the people who create and use this technology to advance equally fast in philosophy, law, logic, sociology, and psychology, so as to be able to cope with these advances. But, knowing how fast technology is moving ahead, the question arises as to whether humans *can* keep pace. And if they don't, who will then become the master—the machine or the human?

This "contest" has been a theme in literature and the arts for the past two centuries. In the folk stories of the nineteenth century, there were the great duels of Paul Bunyan and Babe, the Blue Ox, versus the chain saw and the power locomotive, as well as the duel between John Henry, the Steel Drivin' Man, and the steam riveter. More recently, the projections have gone ahead in time, as related in the classic battle between Dave, the spaceship captain, and his rebellious onboard supercomputer, HAL, in Arthur C. Clarke's *2001: A Space Odyssey.* The question always remains: Who is smarter, faster, more powerful, more dominant—the machine or the human?

What is a matter of constant concern to most people is the fact that what is dreamed and imagined in science fiction very often becomes reality in short order. How it then is distorted or used in ways not originally conceived is what creates the chaos. For example, popular author Michael Crichton penned a novel in which electrodes attached to a man's brain could send him impulses that would diffuse any aggressive or psychotic thoughts he had (*The Terminal Man*). This self-imposed corrective behavior seemed logical and appropriate.

However, in 1996, Peter Rowland, a spokesman for the Picatinny Arsenal in Rockaway Township, New

Jersey, announced that the U.S. Army was sponsoring the development of weapons that used microwaves and lasers to "sense" aggressive psychotic behavior in crowds of people and to protect individuals from attacks by anyone who was emoting thoughts leading to such actions. In a similar theory, a wrist cuff with a vital-sign sensor built into it could detect when a potential aggressor's heart rate increased, blood pressure rose, and body temperature warmed. In response, the wrist cuff would discharge a bolt of electricity so powerful, it would knock down the attacker and render him temporarily incapacitated.

What has happened in this instance is that the technology that was imagined for use in self-control is not being developed that way; instead, its function is being transferred to someone else, so that person can opt to *put* control on another individual.

"What excites me about a device like that," says one law enforcement official, "is its potential to protect women from rapists and protect late-night strollers from muggers. However, what scares me about it is a worry about what will prevent the device from zapping someone who becomes excited by listening to a sports event on a transistor radio or who is excited about getting the news of a raise in pay or who is exhilarated over being in love. Will such a person become an innocent victim of this jolt of electricity just because his or her body temperature rose and the heart started beating faster?"

Again, the good of technology is obvious, but so is its potential consequence.

How Great Is The Advancement?

There is no doubt that advanced technology has a "fun" aspect to it. Standing in front of an automated bank machine in New York that lets you enter your transaction in one of nine languages (including Japanese characters) and then produces your money or transfers your funds in less than ten seconds is "entertaining," as well as functional.

Barbara Brabec, editor of *Home Based Business* newsletter, reports statistics that show that individuals' homes today are virtual arsenals of technology.

Says Brabec, "There are nearly thirteen million fax machines in use at colleges, businesses, government offices, and homes. Some thirty million people have E-mail addresses: students in middle schools where computer labs provide free E-mail access; corporations that provide private E-mail addresses for hundreds of employees within the company; parents and college students who send mail back and forth on a daily basis. These two innovations, alone, have led to the closing of nearly one hundred thousand home-based typing and transcribing businesses. Fewer and fewer people need a third-party stenographer or typist anymore."

Because the number of cellular phone users has increased from less than two million in 1987 to more than twenty million by 1997, the entire country has had to have its area codes rezoned and changed; and the toll-free 800 numbers ran out and had to be supplemented by toll-free 888 numbers or by toll-charged 900 numbers. Additionally, there are twenty-three million people who now carry pagers—plumbers, doctors, sales executives, even illegal narcotics dealers—because they fear being "out of the loop" for even ten minutes.

"If these advances in technology have made people less dependent on third parties," observes Barbara Brabec, "those same advances have also given rise to a new breed of home-based entrepreneur, one who is more focused on providing data, facts, research, polls, background, opinions, studies, projections, and analysis than on providing typing or bookkeeping services."

Brabec says that providing information is what half the workforce is involved in, whether it's by preparing an annual report or telling a traveler what the weather conditions are like in Fargo, North Dakota. Much of this information-disseminating is being done by home-based workers who can elect to work part-time or full-time . . . or full-time at a job away from home and also part-time at a home-based business.

"They say necessity is the mother of invention," explains Brabec, "and that's true in regard to the creation of techno-intensive home businesses. If a person has lost a job due to corporate downsizing, that individual can opt to continue doing his or her old job, only now as a private consultant running his or her own business. Or a person may *want* to work only part-time because of the arrival of a baby or because of health problems, and thanks to computers, fax machines, pagers, cellular phones, and the World Wide Web, that's an option, too."

It has been said that Bill Gates did with home computers what Henry Ford did with the automobile. Each predicted that a day would come when no family would be without one (or more). They were right.

And no one would argue that the automobile has not been a boon to mankind . . . nor dispute that it has caused more deaths and injuries and property damage than most wars. It has been a vicious trade-off.

The question arises, will the computer and its related techno-advances be equally a mixed blessing of benefit and curse? Some analysts are saying a resounding "*yes.*"

James Gleick, in an article titled "Big Brother Is Us," (*The New York Times Magazine*, September 29, 1996, pp. 130-31) showed evidence that one "wound" to society inflicted by technology is a loss of privacy. Once an individual has given away his or her phone number, that person can expect to be bombarded by telemarketing calls; once an address has been offered, an avalanche of junk mail will begin to arrive; once an E-mail code has been shared, a trail of on-line "filler" will begin to be transmitted.

And, according to Gleick, thanks to the enormous memory systems of computers, all of the following information is already known about you: your health history, credit records, marital background, education, employment, every phone call you make, the books you get from the library and the magazines you subscribe to, all of your check or credit card purchases, what is sent to you by electronic mail, where you've traveled by airplane, and how you make use of the World Wide Web when you "surf" it.

Gleick also notes that other forms of technology, ranging from metal detectors at airports to surveillance cameras at banks, are also usurping people's privacy. Do we really need to "expose ourselves" so blatantly? He thinks not. Ironically, however, we usually just abide by it or even encourage it by providing information about ourselves.

WHEN MACHINES MIMIC HUMANS

Beyond the worry over technology watching our every move is an even more awesome challenge: What will we do if we ever are able to create mechanical clones of ourselves? Will we have enhanced our way of life or made ourselves obsolete?

In 1977, when the *Star Wars* trilogy introduced viewers to R2D2 and C3PO, as well as a wide variety of other robots and androids, people began to speculate about whether a time would ever come when robots would function alongside humans in day to day activities. By the late 1980s, when *Star Trek: The Next Generation* introduced viewers to Commander Data—the android who looked, talked, and walked like a human, and who was given a rank and assignment that put it in command *over* humans—it was becoming clear that folks were beginning to accept the idea that one day robots would be "among us."

To a large extent, that day is already here, and it will be completely fulfilled during the new millennium. In 1980, there were about fifteen thousand industrial robots being used in American factories. By 1985, that number had increased to fifty thousand. By 1990 it had increased to five million, and by 1996, the number had surpassed twenty-three million. Then, on April 9, 1997, a Shell gasoline station in Sacramento, California debuted the "Smart Pump." As automobiles entered the gas station—renamed the "customer interface center"—the pump moved next to the driver's door and asked what grade of gasoline the driver desired. The driver answered the question and presented a credit card. The pump then moved to the rear of the car, lowered an extension robotic arm, unscrewed the gas cap, inserted a nozzle, filled the tank, replaced the gas cap, printed a receipt for the customer, then returned the receipt and credit card to the driver. The entire process took less than four minutes' time, and the driver never had to leave the vehicle.

The astounding success of this robot was so immediate, gasoline stations nationwide began to place orders for similar units. This innovation, *alone*, is expected to put another fifteen million robots into daily use by the year 2002.

John Negovetich, president of Tokheim Corporation, one of the world's leading producers of gasoline pumps, announced that Tokheim is developing an even more advanced robot pumping system.

"What we will do is provide automobiles with a special plastic device that will attach to the windshield," said Negovetich. "This device will use radio transmissions to signal the robot as to what make of car is pulling into the station, what grade of gasoline it uses, how to unscrew its gas cap and where it is located, how much gasoline the driver wants, and what credit card will be used to pay for it. Thus, despite rain or snow or hail or sleet, the driver will never have to leave the vehicle. And the robot can adjust for cars, vans, jeeps, or trucks."

THE HISTORY OF ROBOTS

If we seem amazed by predictions that estimate that during the first century of the new millennium there will be literally millions upon millions of new robots functioning in commerce, business, and industry, we need only to be told that the industrial robot did not even exist before 1960, yet today nearly twenty-five million are in use. That, surely, is astounding momentum.

The appeal of robots is obvious. They can work twenty-four hours a day without taking coffee breaks, naps, sick leave, or vacations, or making mistakes. They never report late for work, never request double payment for overtime, never go on strike, never steal from the company, never ask for a benefits package, and once they retire and are no longer of use, they don't ask for a pension.

The desire for mechanical servants is not new. In Greek mythology, the god Zeus grew angry at his son Hephestus, who was the god of forges and blacksmithing. Zeus banished Hephestus from Mount Olympus, crippled him, and forced him to work on Earth. To alleviate his workload, Hephestus forged two female slaves (one from pure gold, the other from silver) and ordered them to do the lifting, carrying, hammering, and loading for him.

More than two thousand years ago in Alexandria, an Egyptian inventor named Hero created dolls and mannequins that could move like humans with the aid of water and paddlewheels.

In the 1700s, woodworker and mechanic Henri Maillardet of France created a large toy that could imitate a little boy working at a school desk. The toy, which looked like a real boy, could move a quill across a paper so well, it could "create" several clever drawings and write three different French poems. This toy still works and is on display in Philadelphia at the Franklin Institute.

Comic-strip heroes from Flash Gordon to Buck Rogers have always had robot companions. Television shows ranging from *Lost in Space* to *The Jetsons* had a robot as a main character. The most popular toy for youngsters in the 1970s was the Transformer, which could change itself from a servant robot to a combat robot. More recent television shows with marketable robots related to the program include the Power Rangers, whose individual smaller robots can convert into sections of what becomes one larger robot. And, with the 1997 rerelease of the "new versions" of the *Star Wars* trilogy, different varieties of the original robot toys from that series have been brought back on the market.

But if toys and cartoons and movies have piqued the imagination with a make-believe world of robots, science and technology have given these imaginings genuine substance. Although the first truly functional robots were not in operation before 1960, their prototype forerunners had existed for at least four decades previously.

The word *robot* is from the Czech word for "compulsory labor," and it was used for the first time as a reference to mechanical beings in a 1921 stage play titled *R.U.R.* (an abbreviation for Rossum's Universal Robots) written by Karel Čapek [pronouced Chop-ick]. The play is set on a remote island where hundreds of thousands of humanoid machines called robots are created to serve as slaves to the humans. In the end, the overworked robots rebel against their creators. (This begs the question of where the robots gained emotions such as revenge, hatred, and anger, which cannot be programmed into a machine, but . . . .)

Probably the first operational robots were developed in 1939 by J. M. Barnett, a research scientist and engineer with Westinghouse Electric & Manufacturing Company. His two creations were Elektro, a nine-foot-tall, 380-pound mechanical man, and his pet mechanical dog Sparko, who could walk, turn his head, wag his tail, sit upon command, and even bark.

Elektro and Sparko were built simply as "crowd

pleasers" for a Westinghouse attraction at the 1939 World's Fair held in New York City. Elektro was oversized and clumsy, and he had to be plugged into a wall circuit at all times. Nevertheless, he could walk forward and backward; he could count to ten on his metal fingers; he could swivel his torso, lift his arms and move his lips; and he could "speak" more than seventy words and expressions (thanks to a phonograph record hidden inside his chest and activated by photoelectric cells).

When visitors to the Westinghouse attraction met Mr. Barnett and asked him if a next generation of robots would be able to do housework or farm labor or factory jobs, Barnett laughed aloud and was quoted as saying, "No engineer would ever be so ridiculous as to imagine that any robot could ever take the place of man."

Fortunately, many other scientists disagreed with Barnett and wound up following his example as a builder of robots rather than one who disdains their capabilities. One such scientist was a biochemistry professor at Boston University named Dr. Isaac Asimov, who, in his 1950 novel called *I, Robot*, coined the term "robotics." In Asimov's science-fiction *Foundation* trilogy (1951–53, with a sequel in 1982), he explained the role, function, need for, and future of robots. Amazingly, although these books were works of fiction, most of the predictions Asimov made became reality between 1960 and 1985. What Asimov conceived mentally in one decade, technicians produced in the next decade.

Two Models of Robots

Today's robots are used to wash skyscrapers, assemble automobiles, clean floors, patrol buildings on the alert for everything from burglars to outbreaks of fire, replicate dinosaurs for movies or for museum displays, and even explore the surface of Mars. Robots can lift, haul, sort, paint, dive, fly, explode, clean, carry, hold, see, hear, grab, transport, record, and tabulate.

There are two basic designs used in creating robots: One is based on human construction, with mechanisms that correspond to hands, legs, ears, and eyes; the other is based on insects, with mechanisms that correspond to protective shells, antennae, biting jaws, and six legs of mobilization and balance.

The robots that borrow their designs from human anatomy do so selectively. That is, it is common for a robot to have arms and fingers (known as manipulators and grippers), yet have no head, neck, torso, or legs.

Robotic manipulators are usually designed to have six degrees of freedom, allowing them to turn in any direction (swivel, rotate, retract, extend, stretch or tilt). They can be created to reach farther than human arms, lift heavier loads, and work under greater extremes of heat or cold. These manipulators can be powered in one of three ways:

1. Compressed air (known as pneumatic power) can be released in blasts through a tube that directs the blast against a rotating piston.
2. Hydraulic liquid can be compressed like air to create the same sort of short blasts of power and thrust, and the liquid can also serve as a coolant and lubricant to keep the machine parts from wearing out quickly.
3. Electric power can be used to turn motors. Sometimes, because electrical units of power can be measured with greater accuracy and can be controlled more effectively, electric motors are the only choice for certain robots, despite the fact that electric motors burn out sooner than do hydraulic units.

The part of the manipulator that corresponds to the human hand can be designed to meet specific job requirements. If the manipulator needs to lift piles of discarded metal for removal, the hand may be a giant magnet. If the manipulator needs to pick up one item and move it from a conveyor belt to a packing box, the hand may have extended grippers that pinch together the way a thumb and forefinger do. If the manipulator must pick up flat panes of glass, its hand may have suction cups on it or a vacuum nozzle. These attachments, known as "end effectors," can also be interchanged to substitute spray paint hoses, drills, or laser cutting tools.

The manipulator and gripper take their orders from a computer that serves as the robot's brain. It was only after computers were being constructed with transistors that they became practical for use in robots, and, thus, robots themselves became practical. The first electronic digital computer was constructed in Philadelphia in 1946 with eighteen thousand glass vacuum tubes. It weighed more than sixty thousand pounds, took up fifteen hundred square feet of warehouse space, required more electrical energy than was needed to supply twenty factories, and required constant maintenance because some of its tubes burned out every few minutes. It could do five thousand sums and one thousand multiplication problems in one minute.

Today, transistors can handle 100 million instructions *per second*, even though they are as small as bacteria ($\frac{1}{24,000}$ of an inch). A robot's computer can be reprogrammed to allow it to do numerous operations. The computer can also be made in such a way that it can test the robot's circuits and moving parts; if it senses some sort of abnormality, it will shut down the computer and send a signal to the maintenance crew to come and repair it. Often, the repair crew brings another robot to assist in repairing the malfunctioning one.

The robot's computer can also be made to respond to sensors. For example, actor Christopher Reeve became a quadriplegic after a fall while horseback riding. Today, he is wheelchair-bound, yet he directs movies and edits scripts and serves as a production coordinator because robotic arms can respond to voice commands he gives them. His voice and his special commands can be programmed into a voice activation unit that causes a robotic arm to turn on a computer screen, turn on a VCR, put a disk in a disk drive, or record a message he wishes to send by phone. Interestingly enough, the sensor recognizes Reeve's voice even when he has a cold, is hoarse, or whispers; yet, it will not respond to anyone else's voice.

Similarly, there are other sensors on certain robots. By using a camera to film its surroundings, the "eyes" of a robot can send the scene before it to the computer, which can map it according to what it knows of the region and can redirect the robot to the next place it should travel.

Tactile sensors help a robot recognize the fragility or strength of a surface it is coming in contact with. By adjusting its grip accordingly, a single robot could pick up a baby bird without hurting it or throw a junked car on its side.

Because the robot is not vulnerable to most of the harmful influences humans must avoid, it can be used to work on radioactive materials, to transport a telephone to terrorists who are holding hostages, to spray-paint in an enclosed environment, to transfer experimental viruses from one test tube to another, or to drill into the side of a mountain where cave-ins are a risk. Robots can go deeper into the ocean than humans can endure. They can enter burning buildings that are too hot for humans to stand and can carry a water hose or flame-suppressant chemicals inside. They can repair space stations from the outside because they do not require air to breathe.

Obviously, the uses for robots are ever-expanding. It is interesting to note that although many of these uses have come into operation only during the past thirty-five years or so, the concepts have been around for many years. (Although he didn't consider it a robot, inventor Thomas Edison created a mechanical doll that could walk and move its arms, in 1890.)

Patterns of development are traceable: In 1801, Joseph Marie Jacquard developed a loom that could weave patterns in silk based on punch cards he created for the loom; in 1954, George Devol invented a workable robotic arm that was programmed by punch cards; in 1976, robotic arms were used in the research conducted by the Viking I and Viking II space probes; and in 1990, a robotic arm retrieved a satellite as big as a railroad car and brought it onboard the space shuttle for repairs. One discovery has always led to advancements in related areas.

ROBOTS IN THE NEW MILLENNIUM

In 1989, the world's first Ph.D. programs in robotics were established at Carnegie-Mellon University. That same year, the National Science Foundation issued a "white paper" that stated that, by the year 2006, the United States would be facing a shortage of 675,000 engineers and scientists. Part of this shortage was based on the idea that uses for robots could be developed rapidly . . . if only there were engineers available to explore the options.

One solution to the problem of a shortage of engineers has been to try to create robots that can program each other and can challenge each other to develop new uses for themselves and other robots. This has not been altogether successful because computers (the brains of robots) do not actually "think." In fact, the official definition of a robot, offered by the Robotics Industries Association, is as follows: "A robot is a reprogrammable, multifunctional machine designed to manipulate materials, parts, tools, or specialized devices, through variable programmed motions, for the performance of a variety of tasks."

Note that nothing in the above definition refers to

thinking, creating, modifying, evolving, developing, or brainstorming. Those challenges yet remain for humans. As early as 1969, small robots that could react to their surroundings via the sensors we discussed earlier were called "thinking robots." Among these was Shakey, a robot built in Palo Alto, California, by engineers at the Stanford Research Institute. Shakey could redirect its actions according to data it registered from its sensors, but it could not actually conceive new ideas.

The primary function of robots has always been to serve their human masters, and to that end, the future has much to offer everyone—and not just factory owners. Here are just of a few of the practical functions robots will be doing around your house and in your community during the next millennium:

Mowing your lawn. Have you observed the wireless fences that hold dogs in yards? They work by underground wires that send painful, high-pitched sounds that only the dog can hear as it gets near them. Thus, the dog stays back away from the wires and remains in its own yard. Using a similar concept, the Poulon Corporation of Shreveport, Louisiana (makers of the Weed Eater), is now manufacturing a mobilized roboticized lawn mower called the "mobot." Homeowners can bury wires around the borders of their yards to signal the mobot to turn and move in another direction. Following such orders, the mobot can move across an entire lawn, cutting grass to an even level. If it bumps into a picnic table, volleyball post, or water sprinkler, it can back up or move around the object.

Washing your car. The same units that serve as drive-through automatic car washes at your local gas station are now being developed for home installation. Designer homes, by the year 2001, will begin to offer this option.

Walking your dog. Small robots similar to vacuum cleaners will be programmed to move along a pre-programmed route through a park or neighborhood, leading a dog by its leash and moving at a pace that is appropriate for the size, weight, and leg length of the dog. The robot will be programmed to make rest stops at certain points, to run the dog for exercise for set time periods, and to bring the animal back home at a specific time.

Retrieving your newspaper and mail. Robots are being designed to stand in front of homes and wait for mail or newspapers to be placed inside them. They then will turn, roll up to the family dwelling, ring the doorbell to announce their arrival, drop the mail through an opening in the door, and then return to the place they started from, next to the street.

Robots are already being used to deliver mail, folders, files, and messages inside buildings. For example, HelpMate is a robot designed by Transitions Research Corporation of Connecticut to work in hospitals. With an encoded map of the hospital in its computer brain, HelpMate uses the elevator to go from floor to floor to deliver medicine, X-rays, food trays, or cleaning supplies from one room to the next. If its path is blocked by a janitor or patient or nurse, HelpMate stops and says, "My way is blocked." Once the person moves, the robot continues its journey.

Guarding your home. Robots on wheels, looking like small golf carts, are now being used by law enforcement agencies to do battle against terrorists, escaped criminals, burglars, or anyone else who may be hiding illegally in a building. One such robot, dubbed RMI, can open doors, use its camera eye to locate adversaries, and then blast them with a water cannon. Experimental versions of such robots are now being tested for home security use. If a homeowner hears a suspicious noise outside, he or she can send the robot to investigate and can see, on an indoor monitor, whatever the robot sees. If a trespasser is spotted, the robot will be able to shoot the person with a paintball of fluorescent paint and put in a 911 emergency mobile phone transmission to the police.

Naturally, these locally used robots won't have the

"drama" attached to them that, say, the Mars Rover will have in 1998 when it is used to explore the surface of Mars; still, they will fulfill a dream we humans have had since the time of the Greek myths: to make robots our on-site servants.

NON-ROBOTIC TECHNOLOGY

If robotic technology seems to be the most exciting of the technological advances ahead of us in the next millennium, it certainly is not the only area for excitement:

The *exoskeleton* is a step-inside suit being developed by the military that will enable a person to jump like a kangaroo, run like an antelope, lift with the strength of a gorilla, and ford streams like a giraffe. Though designed initially for military use, such machines could be used eventually to help the lame to walk, to allow one person to unload trucks and fill warehouses, or to help the police patrol city blocks without the need for squad cars.

At the Massachusetts Institute of Technology, research has led to the creation of a gel that consists of a cross-linked network of long molecule chains held apart by a liquid that keeps the network from falling apart. If light hits this gel (even a light as weak as $\frac{1}{100}$ of a watt), it causes the gel to collapse like ice being instantaneously melted. When the light is turned off, the gel reformulates into its previous consistency. Once this gel substance can be regulated, it will be used to create artificial muscles in the human body that will be able to contract and expand the same way real muscles do, and just as fluidly. Thus, atrophied limbs can be restored for people with body-damaging injuries or diseases.

Affordable videophones are now available and will improve in quality as each year passes. One such unit called ViaTV sells for less than five hundred dollars and can be plugged into a home phone and home TV simultaneously to transmit video images as the phone user talks. Produced by 8x8 Inc. of Santa Clara, California, it comes more than three decades after the concept was originally presented by AT&T at the 1964 World's Fair.

Similarly, beepers and pagers will be carried by everyone in the future. Currently, the Nixxo POP vibrator pager weighs two and one-half ounces, runs off one triple-A battery, and sells for only eighty dollars. Amazingly, it is also an FM radio, even though it is only two inches by one-half inch. The owner can clip it to a belt or purse and listen to the FM radio via earphones while jogging or doing housework or shopping. An auto-scan feature will change channels at the touch of a button. When a beep comes through, the beeper will instantly reduce the volume of the radio and cause the pager to start vibrating.

Thus, on every front—from auto manufacturing to medicine and from communication to lawn care—technology is providing advances meant to make our lives more interesting, more secure, and more carefree. But coming as fast as it is, how can we prepare ourselves for so many changes? There are answers to that question.

WORKING WITH, NOT FOR, TECHNOLOGY

Now is the time to start adjusting to the technoclimate of the year 2000 and beyond. You can go about this in several ways.

Do some focused reading. Rather than fear technology, become acquainted with it. If you are involved in a specific trade, occupation, or career that is technosensitive, make it a point to read the trade journals, company newsletters, industry reports, and scientific announcements. Ask your colleagues about what books they have been reading on advances in your field.

"At Waterfield Mortgage, we have a lending library," reports Becky Teegarten, director of training. "We encourage our employees not only to borrow and read the business-related books we provide, but also to form discussion groups that can meet during lunch hours and coffee breaks. The exchange of ideas provides both new information and motivation for those who take part."

Visit trade shows. Often there will be trade shows, conventions, and demonstration fairs advertised in the business periodicals you read. Consider attending one or more each year. Stop by the various booths; observe the demonstrations of new inventions; pick up flyers and brochures about product breakthroughs. See what's "out there" in your field of interest.

Talk to your clients and customers. Ask the people you serve what new services and products they are most interested in purchasing. If you don't already provide such products and services, find out who does and learn all you can about (and from) your competition. Stay on the cutting edge.

Make better use of the technology you already have. Take an inventory of the machines and innovative products you already have at your office and in your home. Ask yourself how you might be using them to better advantages. Could a fax modem in your computer eliminate the need to print out hard copy for transfer to your fax machine? Could the transfer of your company files to your home computer allow you to take advantage of a "flex time" weekly schedule? Maximize what is already available to you.

Register for continuing education classes. Night school, continuing education courses, and weekend college classes are offered for "nontraditional students" in every city. Get on the mailing list for the semester offerings and find a class you can attend on some aspect of computers, robotics, television, lasers, or applied science. You will be in a class of people of your age group and ability level. You will enjoy the fellow-ship of other people while learning ways to improve your life or business.

. . . And these are just the starting points. You can figure out many other ways to personalize your use of technology. It won't be that difficult. Someone one hundred years ago would never have thought himself capable of adapting to a world in which microwave ovens, gas-powered automobiles, jet airliners, home computers, VCRs, televisions, credit cards, and fast-food restaurants would be the day-to-day norm of things, yet such is the "routine" of your life. You think nothing of it.

So it will be in the future, if you just remind your-self to keep pace.

8: Geopolitical Formations . . . and Reformations

THE GEOGRAPHICAL and political changes that have occurred globally during the past forty years have often been nothing short of stunning.

No sooner do companies like Rand McNally print new maps of a region than everything seems to be changing. Burma has become Myanmar; North and South Vietnam have unified; East and West Germany are also unified; the U.S.S.R. has splintered into separate, independent states.

Similarly, the political landscape has been just as volatile. In Russia, the iron fist was first replaced by *glasnost* and *perestroika*, then replaced entirely by revolution; in America, the Republican landslide victories of Ronald Reagan and George Bush were followed by eight years of Democrat Bill Clinton in the White House; in Ireland the Catholics and Protestants continued to wage their guerrilla war; in Canada, the French-speaking citizens of Quebec tried to form their own nation; and in Hong Kong, the Chinese were given back their deed to the three territories.

This continually evolving geopolitical status has led many people to wonder if global stability will ever be possible in the future. Some feel that, as we near the new millennium, the predictions of "wars and rumors of wars" will be fulfilled as humankind has never before known. Others feel that with such sophisticated defense systems as America's SDI ("Star Wars") system, nuclear war will be rendered obsolete.

Certain experts on these topics have shared their insights for this book. One person is Holly G. Miller, someone with an optimistic outlook on the future of global cooperation among nations.

Holly Miller has spent more than twenty years traversing the globe as travel editor for *The Saturday Evening Post*. She is the author of twelve books and the recipient of more than forty writing awards from Associated Press, the National Association of Press Women, and various travel writing organizations. Her freelance articles appear regularly in *TV Guide*, *Reader's Digest*, and *Indianapolis Monthly*, among many other periodicals.

Miller shared the following responses to key questions about our changing world:

As a person who travels to communist countries regularly, where have you seen the greatest changes during the past five years, and how do such changes serve as evidence of changes yet to come?

MILLER: Prague is the best example I can cite. I've visited what was once Czechoslovakia and is now the Czech Republic. My first visit was about a year before the fall of communism. The city of Prague is magnificent, with its wonderful churches, historic bridges, and lovely homes. However, the contrast between those attractions and the ugly cement apartment buildings erected by the communists was stark. Those newer buildings had no style and seemed to invite the strings of laundry that stretched across the tiny porches and the pitiful, untended shrubs planted before them.

Even the people seemed depressed. They kept their heads down as they hurried through the streets of Prague. There was no lightness or gaiety. I recall attending a private party at which a small group of classical musicians performed. They were wonderfully talented, but as I studied each member, I noticed their threadbare clothes and run-down shoes, and the sorry condition of their musical instruments.

When I went back to Prague in the summer of 1996, everything had changed. Most notably, the *mood* of the city was different. Things were teeming with activity, and the music was back. An open streetcar filled with musicians playing classical pieces careened through the streets. Late into the night, people—especially young people—were out on the streets having fun. Dozens of street vendors were selling their wares on the historic pedestrian bridge that leads to the old city. People looked me in the eye.

The great old buildings were undergoing renovation. Tourists were everywhere. My companions and I no longer had to be accompanied by a guide who wanted to know where each of us had been on our free time. I wandered at will, sticking my head into every interesting cubbyhole I encountered. I hated to leave. This was a solid example of how free enterprise is going to help former communist nations advance quickly. I believe that by the beginning of the new millennium, travel to such nations will not even be considered a novelty any longer—it will be that common an occurrence.

Where on the globe do you find the greatest contrast of very wealthy and very poor people occupying the same country, and will the future change such situations?

MILLER: My recent trips to the Caribbean stand out in my mind in this regard. The native islanders live simply, and often their homes would be considered shanties by U.S. standards. The tourists stay at giant resorts and easily may never have to encounter the local poverty if they never make it a point to take tours around the various islands. I was on Nevis, a small island that is (with its sister island of St. Kitts) a country of its own, having formerly belonged to Great Britain. The Four Seasons resort dominates Nevis and is probably the best thing that has happened to the people there. However, the contrast between rich and poor is extremely evident.

For example, resort officials estimate that in high season, it costs about one thousand dollars a day to enjoy all the amenities of the property. Off-season rates don't fall below six hundred dollars per day. The staff of the resort is all local islanders. So, these people encounter the wealth of the visitors on a daily basis. When they return to their homes at night, they can't help but notice the difference.

And how long does it take someone living in poverty to understand the ways of the wealthy? Well, consider this: When the Four Seasons first opened, the management planned to have employees use three-wheeled bikes to deliver linens and room-service trays to the various hotel rooms. But the employees kept running them into trees or falling off them—they had *never* ridden bikes before! In another example, an employee was sent off-island for training in San Juan, Puerto Rico. When she got to the airport and encountered an escalator, she panicked, screamed and ran. She had to be rescued by airport security. The moving stairs had terrified her.

However, the disparity between the peoples is narrowing. The resort wages are excellent, so as we move into the new millennium, the life style will continue to improve for the islanders. Still, for now, the contrast is very, very evident: The "haves" are being served by the "have nots."

What is going to make world travel easier in the future?

MILLER: "Plastic money. It's almost universal already. Trying to decide how much money to carry and whether to bother with traveler's checks or to try to get local currency has always been a hassle. Now, I carry no more than one thousand dollars in cash for a two-week trip abroad, plus my credit cards. It's smarter to use the credit card as often as possible because it usually has a better exchange rate. Interestingly, the transactions are almost immediate. Also, the credit card helps you keep an accurate record of your expenses for meals, hotels, and local transport.

One of the greatest advantages of using a credit card when abroad is in the purchase of foreign goods that you plan to have shipped back to your home in the States. Previously, the buyer had to pay the money up front, wait for the item to arrive (which wasn't always guaranteed, by the way) and then hope it wouldn't be broken or malfunctioning. Not today, however. Recently, I bought a piece of Swedish crystal while I was in Stockholm. I had to special-order it since none were in stock. It arrived at my home in America three months later, but I was not billed for the item until it was in my possession and verified by me as being exactly what I had ordered.

In the future, what "bugs" in the system still need to be worked out in regard to world travel?

MILLER: Most of them have already been worked out. I remember my first trip to Europe back in nineteen sixty-four, when even nice hotels had shared bathrooms. Now, all rooms have their own facilities. There now are more choices in accommodations, including the popularity of bed and breakfasts where, in places such as New Zealand and Australia, you get a firsthand glimpse of local life and save a few bucks at the same time. Savvy New Zealand farmers add to their income by opening their homes to travelers. Great friendships are fostered this way.

I am expecting more comfort in air travel. The contrast between flying business class and coach ("steerage") is acute. Coach class is terribly uncomfortable by comparison. Business and first class are wonderful, but the prices are prohibitive. The new seven-seven-seven jets are moves in the right direction, with every passenger getting more leg room, his or her own screen for movies or computer use, and extra padding in the seats.

There will have to be some lifting soon of the restrictiveness of the programs for people who fly frequently. The blackout dates and limited use of the so-called bonuses are causing more hard feelings than good public relations. You can expect to see changes in that area, too.

Looking ahead, which tourist spots do you predict will lose appeal and which will gain appeal?

MILLER: Because of our slick methods of mass communications—travel magazines, TV documentaries, newspapers, Internet, travel forums on CompuServe and America Online—a destination cannot live off its good reputation for long. If a few tourists have a bad experience, the world hears about it very quickly.

Poland has a reputation, for example, for having a problem with theft. Spain is even worse. Everyone knows someone who has been "ripped off" in Seville. Too bad, because it's a wonderful city, but my recollections of its beauty are marred by the memory of a friend who had her purse snatched at lunch by a couple of con artists. Prices that are too high can also spoil the reputation of a traveler-friendly destination. For instance, most veteran travelers I know say, "London is wonderful . . . if you can afford it."

Will people be traveling for different reasons in the next millennium?

MILLER: There will be much more business travel because international commerce is increasing each year. The bigger increase, however, will be in people taking several short trips—the extended weekend, the quick jaunt—rather than the one long vacation each summer. Travelers will prefer to be active, rather than just vegetate and be pampered. A lot of grandparents are already hitting the road with their grandchildren.

It makes sense. Mom and Dad are still working, but the kids are at home for the summer and the grandparents are still young enough to enjoy travel (not to mention the fact that they have more money salted away). Adventure travel is becoming very popular, and it comes in degrees. Soft adventuring can be barging through Burgundy in France. Challenging adventure can be joining the crew of a windjammer tall ship. Rigorous adventure can be dogsledding across the Yukon. In the next millennium, the world will be at our doorstep.

GLOBAL PACESETTERS

Globetrotters like Holly G. Miller have shown us that we have gone from Jules Verne's concept last century of traveling *Around the World in 80 Days* to tomorrow's concept of experiencing the world in eighty ways. But does this mean that, from a societal perspective, we will become a global "melting pot"? Several researchers say "no," emphatically.

"Cultures can assimilate aspects of other societies and nations, but that does not mean they will lose their own ethnic, racial, or national identity," explains Dr. Jim Bishop, professor of social studies at Manchester College and an extensive world traveler. "Consider America as an example. Here, we have architectural styles that range from the stucco walls and tile roofs of the Hispanic culture to the Cape Cod designs of England; we have restaurants that provide everything from Hungarian goulash to Chinese egg drop soup; our clothes may be East Indian Nehru jackets one season and Japanese kimonos the next; we drive cars from Germany, Japan, Italy, France, and England; and our language is peppered with every foreign word from *bronco, fiesta, chocolate, siesta, tomato* and *stampede* (Spanish) to *résumé* and *crayon* (French).

Despite all this, do you think an American wouldn't be easy to pick out amidst any group of people?"

Similarly, Dr. Bishop points out, just because Italians eat bratwurst and listen to Mozart, it doesn't make them German, any more than when Canadians eat kielbasa and dance the polka, it makes them Polish. Regional boundaries are going to hold in most cases, and even the World Wide Web's use of English as the universal language is not going to form the earth into the extended family some predicted it would.

Knowing this, it is of interest to look at key points around the globe to see what has been developing and will yet be developing at these locales.

China

In the first two decades of the new millennium, the population of China will increase an estimated 360 million. The available farmland in China has already been maximized. Each day hundreds of thousands of hungry Chinese throng to the big cities seeking work in factories. This has led the economic factions of the state government to put pressure on the military and agricultural factions for concessions. The capital cities are demanding more discipline in the provinces, but the local leaders are finding the masses uncontrollable.

In a *Wall Street Journal* (March 20, 1997) article titled "Asia in 2015," Charles Wolf, Jr., dean of the RAND Graduate School of Policy Studies, predicted, "In 2015, China's gross domestic product will be between $11 and $12 trillion, versus $5 trillion today." Wolf noted that China will have to transfer its wealth from the high-growth eastern provinces to the poorer provinces in the west. He also predicted that cash coming into China from outside nations would slow down. Nevertheless, Wolf said, "China's economy . . . will account for about a quarter of the global product in 2015, which will be twice as large as that of Japan."

China's strides to become part of the world economy were initiated after the 1976 deaths of Mao and Chou. The idolatry of Mao was purged from the land by a new slate of contemporary-thinking politicians. Trade operations were established between China and the United States, Japan, and several European nations. More than one hundred thousand political prisoners were set free from Chinese prisons. Elements of capitalism were encouraged, ranging from bonuses for hard-working factory employees to open competition for entrance to state universities.

The decade of the 1980s saw China, under the communist leadership of Chairman Deng Xiaoping, establish industrial liaisons with other countries in an effort to make China's leading cities convert from a produce economy to a technical- and scientific-driven economy. This also exposed the people, however, to Western thought and ideology.

On May 4, 1989, more than one hundred thousand students and common laborers staged a peace march in Beijing. They set up tents and settled down for a long stay in Tiananmen Square. They had severely misjudged the tolerance level of the government, however. Martial law was declared, and on June 3 and 4, troops attacked the protesters, killing anywhere from one thousand to six thousand of them, injuring more than ten thousand others, and arresting an additional twelve thousand. A public trial was held for thirty-one of the chief instigators, and all were found guilty and were executed. New laws were established that forbade any such future demonstations.

With the country's population exceeding 1,226,000,000 people, the government of China has been encouraging its couples to limit themselves to one child. As a whole, the country now has a density of 340 people per square mile. Its president is Jiang Zemin (since 1993) and its premier is Li Peng (since 1988). It maintains a standing army of approximately 2½ million troops.

Although the Chinese fought against American soldiers in Korea in 1950, two decades later the United States supported the admission of China to the United Nations (although the U.S. did not support the expulsion of Taiwan from the U.N. at the same time).

President Nixon visited China in 1972, and the countries established cultural exchange offices in each other's capitals in 1973. On December 15, 1978, the United States formally recognized the People's Republic of China as the only legitimate government of China, and the next year, formal diplomatic relations were established between the two nations. Although human rights violations have continued, the United States has not revoked its most-favored-nation trading status from China, and in September 1996, Mrs. Hillary Rodham Clinton went to China to attend the United Nations' Fourth World Conference on Women. This came in the wake of tension earlier that year when China staged military exercises off the coast of Taiwan, resulting in the deploying of two U.S. naval war groups (led by USS *Nimitz* and USS *Independence*) into that area.

Though overpopulated and still technologically behind most other advancing nations, China will simply have to be a "player" to be reckoned with in the next millennium. Its land mass, population, and developing economy will force the country's presence on the rest of the world.

Bosnia

On November 24, 1995, in Bad Kreuznach, Germany, U.S. Secretary of Defense William J. Perry addressed the officers and NCOs of the 1st Armored Division. The Bosnian peace agreement had been signed in Dayton, Ohio, just three days earlier. NATO had decided to commit sixty thousand troops (twenty-thousand of them being Americans) to the Republic of Bosnia and Herzegovina in an effort to invoke martial law in this war-torn nation. It was Secretary Perry's job to explain to the troops why they were going to war.

"The United States has vital political, economic, and security interests in Europe," said Perry. "The war in Bosnia threatens these interests." He explained that after four years of civil war, resulting in 200,000 deaths and two million refugees, it was time to put an end to the madness. By sending in U.S. bombers and ground troops to enforce peace, the various factions were being forced to call a cease fire. "None of the parties . . . would have been willing to sign the peace agreement without an American commitment," Perry continued, "and one of the parties has already publicly stated that they would withdraw from the agreement if that commitment is not met."

What led to this civil war in a country of fewer than 2,600,000 people, and why it should upset all the members of the North Atlantic Treaty Organization dates back to the early 1900s. In 1918, Bosnia was made a province of Yugoslavia, and when the Yugoslavian constitution was revised in 1946, Bosnia was united with Herzegovina as a federated republic.

On February 29, 1992, the parliament of Bosnia and Herzegovina declared independence, and on April 7, the new nation was officially recognized both by the United States and the European Union. The nation's population consisted 40 percent of Serbs, 38 percent of Muslims and 22 percent of Croatians. Three-way battles raged among all factions. The ethnic Serbs were against the move for independence, and, in open rebellion, their forces slaughtered tens of thousands of Muslims and Croats; those they didn't kill, they attempted to expel from the country as part of an "ethnic cleansing." In retaliation, the Bosnian Croats and Muslims signed a confederation agreement on March 18, 1994, after having already agreed to a cease fire of hostilities against each other. By then, however, the Serbs had control over three-quarters of the territory of Bosnia.

The Serbs had surrounded the capital city of Sarajevo in 1994, and they held it in siege until, in 1995, massive air strikes from NATO forces caused the Serbs to withdraw on September 15. In an aggressive counterattack, the Croatian and Muslim forces drove the Serbs back off a third of their land holdings. Seeing they were outgunned, the Serbs agreed to come to the peace table.

In Paris, on December 14, 1995, the Serbs signed the agreement that had been drawn up in Dayton, Ohio. It allowed a three-party government and designated 49 percent of the land mass of Bosnia to the Serbs. Formal elections were held on September 14, 1996, which brought into office a collective presidency consisting of Alija Izetbegovic [Muslim], Kresimir Zubak [Croat], and Momcilo Krajisnik [Serb]. After the elections, NATO withdrew fifteen thousand of its original sixty thousand ground forces (leaving sixteen thousand U.S. troops still in-country). The United Nations began holding war crimes trials in late 1996 and early 1997 to investigate reported atrocities.

President Clinton has affirmed that U.S. troops will continue to support the NATO police action in Bosnia; this implies that, for the remainder of this century, the peace in Bosnia may remain a forced peace.

The Irish Republic and Northern Ireland

When on February 9, 1996, the Irish Republican Army initiated terrorist acts after a self-imposed cease fire that had been in effect since August 31, 1994, world observers began to wonder if the conflict in Ireland would ever end. Even now, with more than 3,200 civilians killed in bombings and assassinations since 1969, the underground war continues. The future of this region is expected to be one of factions of Catholics and Protestants continuing to do battle.

To understand the events that led to these dissensions, one need only go back to 1920. In that year, the

British Parliament separated the six counties of Ulster in the northeast corner of Ireland (with Belfast and Londonderry) from the twenty-six southern counties of southern Ireland. In 1922, both of these British "dominions" were asked to decide on their alliances: Northern Ireland remained with the United Kingdom, but the southern counties became a free state in dominion status. Then, on December 29, 1937, Ireland (*Eire*, in Irish) proclaimed itself an independent democratic state.

Conditions remained somewhat stable until December 21, 1948, when Ireland proclaimed itself a republic and announced it was withdrawing from the British Commonwealth. The next year, the British agreed to this, with the proviso that the six most northern counties of Ulster remain under British control. The government of the newly formed Irish Republic rejected this concession, and terrorist groups began to plant bombs throughout England in an effort to force the British to release their hold on Ulster. Since then, the British have attempted to work out peaceful agreements for a united Ireland, but religious factions distrust each other's motives. In Northern Ireland, the population is 67 percent Protestant, whereas in the Irish Republic it is 94 percent Catholic.

On December 15, 1993, the Irish and British governments announced that they had agreed to resolve the Northern Ireland reunification issue through peace talks and treaties. So, the IRA and other factions agreed to "give peace a chance." However, the peace talks made virtually no progress, so in early 1996 the IRA resumed its acts of terror, and the British troops and Protestant loyalists retaliated with martial law, curfews and trade sanctions.

Optimists point out that the peace talks are still going forward. Pessimists point out that since the Protestants and Catholics haven't been able to coexist as neighbors, it isn't likely they will be able to cohabit as countrymen.

Canada

On October 30, 1995, by an incredibly narrow margin of 50.6 percent to 49.4 percent, the citizens of Quebec voted not to separate themselves from the rest of Canada. Tears of agony were shed in one camp of voters and tears of relief in the other camp.

However, according to pollster Allan Gregg, the defeat of the Separatists' agenda should not be taken as a signal that a unified Canada exists now and forever. In fact, in an article titled "Can Canada Survive?" (*Maclean's*, December 1995) Gregg reported, "Today, almost one in three Canadians—and every second Quebecer—reports a belief that by the end of the decade, our nation, as we know it, will cease to exist."

After seemingly endless and fruitless efforts to achieve constitutional accord, English-speaking Canada appears to be losing its resolve to embrace Quebecers and their aspirations. The majority of Canadians, Quebecers included, felt that the huge federalist rally in Montreal just before the referendum helped to attract voters to the "no" side; but Separatists, far from growing weary, are increasingly convinced that sovereignty is inevitable. Gregg noted that English-speaking Canada holds an almost unshakable view that Canada is composed not of two founding groups [English and French] but ten equal provinces, with Quebec entitled to absolutely nothing that shouldn't be available to all.

And in the next millennium? Allan Gregg's recent polls show that 64 percent of the people in Quebec believe that a majority of the people will vote to withdraw from Canada by the year 2000, even though only 38 percent of the people in the other nine provinces agree with this.

Responding to questions for this book, researcher and reporter Christa Bartlett of Quebec noted, "Going from sea to sea, Canada is a unique collection of diverse entities. In the west, there are Eskimos and Indians who are as native to this land as the English and French descendants. We have English, French and a variety of other languages spoken in the provinces. We have industrialists and farmers and oil drillers and miners and fishermen and ranchers. We have huge metropolises, such as Toronto with four million people, Montreal with three million, Vancouver with two million and Ottawa-Hull with one million, yet we also have thousands of tiny villages and camps. My point is, the Quebec question has to go beyond the language problem, for Canadians have long ago learned to live with cultural differences."

Be that as it may, splinter groups will be dividing sections of Canada for themselves in the final years leading to the new millennium. For example, voters in the Northwest Territories passed a referendum in May 1992 that will set aside 136,493 square miles of their land strictly for the Inuit people; possession is set to be completed by the last months of 1999.

Politically, Canada has been mercurial. After eight years in office as prime minister, Brian Mulroney resigned on February 24, 1993. In October, the Conservative Party, which had enjoyed a long reign of dominance in the House of Commons, lost all but two of the 295 House seats. Jean Chrétien became the new prime minister, the first Liberal since 1984, following Kim Campbell's brief seven-month stint at that job.

Analysts predict that Canada will enjoy a lull in its political upheavals for two or three more years, but then the situation in Quebec will once again arise, bringing with it all the other issues of language, territoriality and political party realignment. More sparks are yet to fly.

Republic of South Africa

Despite the fact that the Constitutional Court of South Africa on September 6, 1996, rejected that country's newly drafted constitution, evidences abound that this nation of forty-two million people will soon evolve as a "power" to be reckoned with during the new millennium. It is the world's largest producer of platinum, gold, and chromium, and it has vast quantities of iron, coal, tin, diamonds, copper, uranium, and nickel, all of which are desperately needed in global commerce. With a new government formed under President Nelson Mandela, South Africa is primed to make advances that will benefit its people and promote its prosperity.

The word *apartheid*, meaning strict segregation of nonwhites (particularly blacks) from rights in voting, holding office, owning land and companies, marrying out of their race, and living in housing areas dominated by whites, had its origins in South Africa. The country's policies and traditions date back to the beginning of the 1600s, when Dutch traders drove the Zulu and Swazi natives away from the Cape of Good Hope. After nearly two centuries of dominance in the region, the Dutch were driven north in 1806 when the British seized the Cape.

At first, the Dutch were content to form two separate republics to the north, the Orange Free State and the Transvaal. However, when it was learned in 1867 that the southern region of Africa was laden with diamonds (gem-quality), the Dutch began to covet the territory they had lost. Tension increased in 1886 when it was further discovered that the region was rich with deposits of gold. In 1899, the Boers (Dutch) declared war in Africa against the on-site British. Battles raged for nearly four years until the British won the war and, as part of the spoils, took control of all Dutch republics and territories.

In 1910, the British united these various adjacent colonies and republics into the Union of South Africa and held strong rule there until May 31, 1961, when a referendum declared by the local government announced that the newly formed nation of the Republic of South Africa had completely withdrawn from the British Commonwealth.

The National Party had taken control of the government back in 1948 and had officially sanctioned the policy of apartheid. Within a decade, however, the black, Asian, and mixed-race minorities were talking rebellion, so 13 percent of the land of South Africa was designated as "Bantu land" for the locals as of 1959. This did not appease the nonwhite population, so after the creation of the republic in 1961, the white politicians created an "Indian Advisory Board," although it had no real power. As a further act of contrition, the white government created a Coloured People's Representative Council in 1969, but it, too, proved only to be window dressing.

By the decade of the 1970s, it was evident that the whites were taking the wealth from South Africa for their own gain and were sharing none of it with the nonwhites. Violence was reported in numerous townships, and, in 1976, more than six hundred Bantus were killed when they staged a riot against the national government. During the 1980s, an additional ten thousand people in the Zulu region were killed in fighting between forces of the African National Congress (ANC) and the South African defense forces.

In November 1983, a new constitution was adopted that allowed whites, Asians, and mixed-breed ("coloured") people the right to vote, but not the 70 percent of the population that was black. In August 1985, the United States invoked economic sanctions against South Africa. Bishop Desmond Tutu, a recipient of the Nobel Peace Prize, encouraged other Western nations to follow suit, which eleven did in 1986. However, rather than yield to pressure, South African troops on May 19, 1986, made all-out attacks on ANC guerrilla strongholds in the neighboring nations of Zambia, Botswana, and Zimbabwe.

When combat failed to effect change in South Africa, the residents united in a three-day strike (June 6–8, 1988) in which two million blacks refused to report to work in the mines, the civil departments, private stores and shops, transportation operations, and farms. This shut down the nation and showed the power of the nationals. Fourteen months later, P. W. Botha resigned from office after eleven years as president, and was replaced in September 1989, by Frederik W. de Klerk, who promised "evolutionary change in government."

President de Klerk lifted the ban on the ANC in 1990; he released black nationalist leader Nelson Mandela from prison (after twenty-seven years); he saw to it that the Separate Amenities Act was repealed; he proclaimed an end to apartheid laws; and he agreed to repeal the Race Registration Law. In 1993, the existent political parties agreed on the tenets of a new constitution that would allow citizens of all races to vote. Elections held from April 26–29, 1994, gave Nelson Mandela a landslide victory as the new president (62.7 percent of the vote). The following year, Mandela appointed Bishop Tutu to head a panel to investigate allegations of human rights violations and genocide during the era of apartheid.

In March 1997, President Mandela traveled to the United States to meet with President Clinton to discuss new avenues of commerce, trade, tourism, and military cooperation between the two nations. Political analysts predicted that liaisons such as this would pave the way for the Republic of South Africa to "come into its own during the twenty-first century."

Mexico

No nation has had a closer relationship, both geographically and politically, with the United States during the past five years than has Mexico. From a positive view, that has included the ratifying of the 1994 North American Free Trade Agreement (NAFTA), the establishment of hundreds of American-owned factories and businesses in Mexico, and the supplying of vast quantities of crude oil, coffee beans, and other commercial goods to the U.S. From a negative view, it has meant the influx of thousands of illegal aliens crossing the border from Mexico into Texas and California, massive financial support in 1995 from the United States to keep the Mexican currency from collapsing, and the threat of border wars as two guerrilla factions—the Zapatista National Liberation Army and the Popular Revolutionary Army—continue to stage uprisings (since 1994) against the federal government of Mexico.

Mexico City currently ranks as the most populated city in the world, with some fifteen million residents within or around the city limits. As a nation, Mexico's 756,000 square miles are home to close to one hundred million people, the vast majority of whom are either unemployed or underemployed. Poverty abounds in most of the country's thirty-one states.

Though the nation produces corn, beans, rice, wheat, cotton, and tomatoes, only 11 percent of its land can be tilled, and many foreign countries refuse to import Mexican produce. Mexico has a reputation for poor sanitation, as evidenced in April 1997, when strawberries shipped from Mexico to California and later distributed in a U.S. school lunch program caused outbreaks of hepatitis A in more than two hundred elementary students in eleven U.S. states.

The relationship between the United States and Mexico has a long history of love-hate experiences. The U.S.-Mexican War of 1846–48 resulted in Mexico losing what today is New Mexico, Arizona, Texas, and California to the United States. Nevertheless, when French military troops forced an Austrian archduke on the Mexican people as their ruler (Maximilian I, 1864–67), U.S. threats of invasion forced the French to withdraw and turn Mexico back over to the Mexicans.

Though ruled by dictators for most of the late 1800s, Mexico adopted a constitution on February 5, 1917, that provided more voting power to the common people. Since first coming into office in 1929, the Institutional Revolutionary Party (PRI) has been the dominant political force in Mexico, right down to the most recent swearing-in of PRI candidate Ernesto Zedillo Ponce de Léon as president on December 1, 1994.

Mexico is a land of great contrasts: Although it provides free (and compulsory) education for its citizens, no one has to attend school after age twelve; although one out of every six Mexicans owns a color television, there is only one hospital bed per every 1,400 people in the country; although it attracts $6.5 billion annually in tourism, the reason for this is that the Mexican peso is valued at less than one-seventh the value of the U.S. dollar.

Such contrasts are not lost on U.S. observers. Whereas Mexico represents a source of unlimited cheap labor for plants that open there for automobile construction, each such opening takes thousands of new jobs away from higher-paid union workers in America. Likewise, whereas the millions of Mexican people who are eager to own the luxury goods produced in America provide a vast market for the selling of U.S. products, the need to support the Mexican currency by huge loans to the Mexican government only serves to increase tax burdens and fuel inflation in America. It is a circular problem that has no immediate solution.

The most optimistic speculations regarding Mexico's future are that the open trade being stimulated by NAFTA and similar trade alliances will provide three benefits: 1) as more U.S. and Canadian businesses are established in Mexico, the Mexican unemployment rate will fall, the economy will improve, and the poverty will lessen; 2) as mass amounts of goods produced at cheaper rates arrive from Mexico to the U.S. and Canada, those goods will be made available at much lower prices and, thus, will decrease inflation and make more products available to more consumers; and 3) as Mexican workers increase their own standard of living, they will want to buy goods that are made exclusively in the U.S. and Canada, thus raising the demand for locally produced materials and goods.

Should this prove true, Mexico will emerge in the new millennium as a strong economic, social, political, and industrial nation.

SUMMARY

From a world view, we can echo Dickens in proclaiming it to be the best of times, the worst of times. The increased ease of travel and improved tourist conditions reported by Holly G. Miller and others make the planet a traveler's delight. Nevertheless, ongoing rebellions everywhere from Ireland to Mexico show the world still to have its danger zones.

What cannot be denied, however, is that phenomenal geopolitical changes—the tearing down of the Berlin Wall, the breakup of the USSR, the takeover of black rule in South Africa, the reclaiming of Hong Kong by China, the population explosion in Mexico—have created a climate of wonder and amazement. If it is true that no one can give a precise prediction as to how the countries of the world will be revamped in the new millennium, it is equally true that no one can deny that "status quo" is no longer the standard in either geography or global politics. Changes are coming that will rival even the most startling occurrences we have already experienced.

9: Families, Societies, and the Global Village

IF YOU tune in to one of the family channels and catch some old reruns of *Leave It to Beaver* or *The Brady Bunch* or *Ozzie and Harriet*, or even the earliest episodes of *The Cosby Show*, you get a sense of momentum. That is, as the episodes progress through the years, the children grow up before you, they enter new life phases with the accompanying trials and lessons learned, and they use these new experiences to prepare themselves to, in time, emulate the life styles of their parents.

Said another way, the mission of the parents has always been to make themselves unnecessary. If children have been reared in a home where they've been told and taught that they must earn good grades, work summer jobs, dress nicely, show proper manners, and learn to stand on their own, they, too, will one day be able to get married, buy a home and car and nice furniture, have children, and enjoy "the good life."

For a long time, that worked. Today, however, the children are far less eager to leave this environment. Many of them wish they could just go on being the child and let their parents care for them the rest of their lives. Some have gone out into the cruel world and found it too inhabitable (or nowhere near as comfortable as it was back home), so they have moved back in with their aging parents. This has thrown the whole cycle of parent-child-grandchild out of synchronization.

Research reported in *Current Thoughts & Trends* (July 1996, p. 11) reveals that in the early 1970s, only 15 percent of adults aged twenty-five or older were still living at home with their parents. By 1990, that had increased to 21 percent and was still rising. Many of these "children" had jobs unrelated to their chosen career fields. More than half were providing no financial support for the parents who were taking care of them. Instead, they were spending their earnings on things for themselves—stereo systems, sporty cars, fancy clothes, dates at nice restaurants, and modern computer equipment.

When questioned about why they returned home, they gave varied answers: "My marriage went sour, and I had no one else to take care of me" ... "I had an apartment, but I was lonely" ... "I quit working for the company I was at because it had a lot of old guys who wouldn't retire, so there was no room for advancement there" ... "I went kind of crazy with my credit cards and couldn't make my rent payments, so they evicted me" ... "I was living with someone, and we decided it just wasn't meant to be" ... "I could pay my rent and utilities, but I had none of the extras I was used to at home, like a swimming pool and sun deck, microwave oven, big-screen TV, VCR, stereo system, oversized closets, and a garage for my car."

Not all young adults who retreat home are doing so with the sole idea of bilking their parents. Some return for an extra year or two until they pay off their college loans. Some just want a place to stay for a year or so until they can get their wedding plans in order and put aside enough cash for a down payment on a home. Still others don't want to invade their parents' living space; they just want to use their former bedroom as a place to store things until they return from a tour of duty in the military or get settled into a new job in a different state.

No matter what the justification is, however, this returning of the chick to the empty nest is still altering the way society has long perceived how the cycle of one generation evolving into the next should be done. As one man in his late sixties explained it, "I've got a twenty-three-year old son and a twenty-nine-year old daughter back living with my wife and me. Both are college graduates and they are in excellent health, yet they show no effort to strike out on their own. It's as though they assume that one day we'll die and leave them the house and furniture and cars, and they'll be able to just go on living at home. But I ask you, who is going to pay for the utilities and insurances and gasoline and new tires and roof repair and yard maintenance if there's no cash coming in? They don't seem to think about that. And what's worse, my wife and I had always expected our kids to take care of us in our old age, not us having to continue taking care of them. Where did we get off track?"

And what of the traditionalists? When the series *Leave It to Beaver* was brought back to television as a sequel of itself, this time with Wally and Beaver as adults with families of their own, the scenario was more reflective of life as it is today. As a dad, Beaver was a single parent, recently divorced from his "liberated" wife who ran off to "find herself." Beaver's mother, June Cleaver, was a widow, her husband having given his all to corporate America and then having died prematurely.

Why was their traditional image of middle-class America altered so drastically? Because what happened to Beaver Cleaver had happened to most of America.

America has the highest divorce rate of any country in the world, and that rate is rising by 3 percent annually. Lifetime commitment was genuine for June Cleaver, who stayed with Ward until he died; for Beaver's wife, it was commitment until one of the two of them found something better.

The original *Beaver* series ran in the 1950s. People of that era could identify with this nuclear family of dad, mom, and two kids. However, by 1970, there were more single-parent (or solo adult with no off-spring) families than there were two-parent traditional (nuclear family) units. Then, by 1990, there were only 700,000 two-parent families in America, a mere 26 percent of the family units. The "traditional" family had become a widowed or divorced woman living alone (or with children she was trying to support), or a family with grown children who still lived at home, or young unmarrieds living alone at college or in small apartments while they pursued whatever career opportunities might be available.

"The really unfortunate thing about this situation is that it works to undermine the traditional family structure even further," says Rev. Timothy Franklin, a pastor who specializes in family counseling in Bryan, Ohio. "I say that because people who live alone or who still live [as adults] with their parents feel no obligation to support family-oriented institutions. They will vote 'no' on referendums calling for increased taxes for better schools, better day-care facilities, increased medical research to cure children's illnesses, or anything that doesn't directly improve their own personal lives. And since there are so many of these people, their voting power is substantial. As they allow family services to decrease, the family units decrease accordingly, and the problem feeds on itself. Then people come to counselors such as myself and ask, 'Why don't these kids today grow up with any civic pride, any sense of community respect, any motivation to make something of themselves?' Well, to that, all I can respond is, 'What goes around, comes around.' "

Debates continue to rage regarding the need for concern over these evolutions of the modern family. During the late 1980s, then–Vice President Dan

Quayle made bold statements regarding the need to preserve the traditional family unit. He claimed that everything from crime to suicide could be lowered if families could go back to the dad-*and*-mom cycle. He was ridiculed by liberal-thinking individuals who counter-claimed that there was no basis for his claims. One popular television show—*Murphy Brown*, starring Candice Bergen in the title role—went so far as to have its main character have a child purposefully out of wedlock and even mocked Vice President Quayle both on- and off-screen.

Subsequent formal research conducted by private institutions and the U.S. government revealed that what Mr. Quayle had been saying did, in fact, have statistical research to support it. This led numerous newspapers, and even the prestigious *Atlantic Monthly* magazine [April 1993], to run headlines proclaiming such apologies as "Dan Quayle Was Right." It did not greatly alter the habits of most Americans, however.

Although Mr. Quayle and others gave strong endorsements to the two-parent family, the high-profile cases of single-mom families garnered far more interest during the 1990s. Singer and movie star Madonna Ciccone gave birth to Lourdes Maria out of wedlock in 1996. Madonna announced publicly that the father of the child was Carlos Leon, Madonna's physical fitness trainer and close companion, but the couple did not marry. The accompanying publicity proved to be a boost for Carlos Leon's career, including the landing of a recurring role in a popular television series.

Numerous other celebrities have also opted, by birth or by adoption, to become single moms, including Diane Keaton (*First Wives Club, Father of the Bride*), Robin Givens (television actress, model, and former wife of former heavyweight champ Mike Tyson), Rosie O'Donnell (*A League of Their Own, The Rosie O'Donnell Show*), Sheena Easton (multiple Grammy Award-winning recording artist), and Michelle Pfeiffer (*Dangerous Minds, Batman Returns*).

It is not surprising that many of the high profile single moms are women with celebrity status: An independent adoption can cost between twenty-one and twenty-eight thousand dollars. (Rosie O'Donnell was able to adopt her son, Parker Jaren, when he was only two days old.) Other women became single moms the more traditional way—by giving birth to babies and keeping them. The stigma that once accompanied this seems to be waning: In 1960, only 13,600 single women under the age of thirty-five gave birth to out-of-wedlock babies; in 1992, that number had risen to more than 63,000 (and this did not include the single women who had adopted children nor the single women who had been impregnated by in vitro fertilization).

Often, single women who wish to adopt a child find that they are offered only special-needs children or older children. This is not because the adoption agencies consider these women to be unfit to care for a baby, but because birth parents often make a condition for adoption that their infant go to a two-parent family. Bethany Christian Services of Grand Rapids, Michigan, is the largest adoption agency in America. It reports that 41 percent of the adoptions of older or special-needs children that it handles in Michigan are for single women.

"There is a lot of statistical research to prove that children from two-parent homes do benefit in a wide variety of ways," notes Bill Herald, former police chaplain to the Illinois chapter of the Sheriff's Association. "However, you have to get pragmatic and ask yourself which situation is worse: a child with one excellent parent or a child with no parents at all. In that light, I can tell you from personal experience, both as a lawman and as a minister, the child with one parent is better off. That child has someone who shows up at PTA meetings, who sits and watches TV with the youngster, and who is there when he or she has a scraped elbow or knee. That's important in a child's psychological and social development."

Chaplain Herald also points out that single parenthood is no easy life. "If you don't have a co-parent, you wind up having to hire baby-sitters every time you need to go shopping or on a date or to attend an event with adult friends. You have to find day care for when you are working. You often forfeit vacations. You have no one to share the responsibilities with of getting up for the 2 A.M. feeding or helping with homework or giving baths or teaching lessons in football. Single parents have to ask themselves how much of their desire to be parents is based on an idea of snuggling a cuddly little infant and how much is based on genuine knowledge that they will have to feed, clothe, educate, entertain, protect, house, insure, nurture, and support that child for at least two decades."

Statistics show that whereas in 1960, only 5 percent of children were born to unwed mothers in America, by 1996 it was 34 percent. This seems to be a "middle ground" from a global perspective, for in Sweden more than 50 percent of all births are to unwed mothers, while in Japan less than 1 percent of births are to unwed mothers. France and England are also approximately at 33 percent like the United States, but Germany is at only 15 percent, while Denmark is at 47 percent.

Even accounting for wanted pregnancies, aborted or not, these percentages send two messages: one, that the traditional family of the pre-1960s has been remolded in a variety of ways; and two, that people, even when they do not opt for life in a nuclear family, still have an innate desire to "belong."

TRIBE, FAMILY OR GOING SOLO?

There is no doubt that all people have a need to feel accepted, to feel part of a greater group. In the 1960s, the songs proclaimed such bonding with "I'm In with the In Crowd." Barbra Streisand told us, "People who need people are the luckiest people in the world." The Beach Boys admonished everyone to "be true to your school," and countless other singers extolled the merits of love-ins, rallies, and communes. The message was, either you belong to some larger unit, or else you are doomed.

Too often, the larger units didn't live up to their expectations or potential, however. This became very evident in the subsequent decade of the 1970s. For example, one of the biggest communes, founded in Jonestown, Guyana, by the Rev. Jim Jones, ended in a mass suicide (912 deaths) in 1978.

Similarly, being true to one's school proved laughable when academic standards were continually lowered to the point of awarding a graduation "certificate" for "showing up for four years" as opposed to a high school diploma for academic achievement.

The love-ins led to record high cases of venereal disease and the development of a no-cure sexual killer labeled Acquired Immunodeficiency Syndrome (AIDS).

Nevertheless, people still had the aforementioned innate need to bond. If this need could not be met by being part of a traditional family, then it would be met vicariously by the creation of gangs, with gang colors and protected "turf." Modern America, for all its sophistication, found itself reverting to tribal territoriality in the 1970s and 1980s, particularly in the largest cities.

By the 1990s, this had permeated all aspects of living. The war was on. In a 1996 poll taken by *Brigade Leader* magazine, 25 percent of surveyed teens said they feared regularly for their safety when at school, and 28 percent said they knew of students in their grades who came to school with knives, blackjacks, or guns.

Nevertheless, the school was their primary bonding experience, for three out of five students said they spent less than an hour a week with their mothers and four out of five said they spent less than an hour a week with their fathers. A full 68 percent of these students said they virtually never talked to their parents about school, dating, money, hobbies, friends, food, health, entertainment, or future plans.

There is an obvious irony here. On the one hand, we have a generation of young people who understand isolation and even identify with it: they can sit alone for hours in front of a television or VCR or a computer screen, never speaking to anyone or leaving the room. On the other hand, there is a basic need to bond with others that has led most teens to become sexually active by age fourteen, to "party" and "get wasted" on drugs or alcohol with friends, or possibly to join a gang or cult.

"It seems a contradiction in beliefs," admits Michael Smith, professor of journalism at Taylor University, "but my work as a reporter and teacher shows me that there is a rational pattern of thought among these young people."

Prof. Smith explains, "To understand why these young folks think and act the way they do, you must begin with the knowledge that most of them are very distrustful of authority in any form. They don't like institutions. They haven't been able to rely on their parents. Teachers and police officers and ministers are viewed as disciplinarians who dole out punishment if certain rules—ones not devised by or agreed to by the young people themselves—are not strictly adhered to. Most of these youngsters are antiestablishment because the establishment has seldom been on their side."

Smith believes the cynicism and disillusionment of this younger generation has evolved to a point at which each young person seeks only a sense of immediate significance.

"If at all times the only thing you are asking yourself is, 'Of what value is this to me at this very moment?' then you will do whatever it is that is of significant value to you at that instant. If you can smoke pot and not risk getting caught, you'll do it. If you can have sex with a willing partner, you'll do it. If you can rent a video and sit alone and watch it, you will do so. If you can be part of a gang or cult where nobody puts rules on you, just accepts you for who you are, you're going to join that group. If you can sit in front of a computer and pretend to be a galaxy warrior, you'll do it even if it's only virtual reality and not a true experience at all."

When asked why all young people are not this way, Prof. Smith cites the example of role models.

"You've got to remember that there are millions of young people in this country who are attending private schools where gang activity is not present. These students often come from upper-class families who stress academic achievement, personal accountability, and strong moral values. Even many of the students in public schools come from two-parent families where they are made to feel a significant part of the family. They grow up believing it is 'the right way,' and they later want to copy it. Single-parent families often provide excellent role models by interacting with grandparents, coaches, church youth leaders, 4-H or YMCA or YWCA leaders or Scouting. Not all young people are extremists who seek either solitude or gang activity."

Whether extremists or more traditional, the youth of today are, indeed, different. Understanding them requires some special insights. Bob Hostetler, best-selling author of such books for teens as *They Call Me A.W.O.L.* and *Adventures in Vertical Living*, suggests six specific ways that young people of the next millennium can be reached.

"You first need to know their world," says Hostetler, "and by that I mean their fears, their likes and dislikes, their friends, and their interests. Secondly, you've then got to enter their world. You can actually shock a young person by proving you recognize his or her favorite song on the radio or that you can beat him or her at a favorite video game.

"Third, you need to work on relationships. Young people still go in for those seemingly 'corny' activities like canoe trips, raft rides, camping, road rallies, and sports events. They want a chance to bond with adults in ways the Walkman and Nintendo can't provide. One parent I know has been reading books aloud to his two children since they were tots. They are now in their late teens, yet this is still a family activity. You cannot believe how many classics by Charles Dickens, Jack London, Henry James, and Bret Harte they have completed over the years."

Hostetler continues, "Fourth, adults need to cater to the short attention spans of young people. Several five-minute chats will be more effective than a half-hour speech. Keep in mind that in the previous generation, everything moved in slow motion. If you turned on the television, nothing happened until the tubes heated up; today, with one touch of the remote control, the set is instantaneously on. Back one hundred seventy years ago, people were content to wait five days for a stagecoach to arrive. Today, they get ticked off if they miss one section of a revolving door.

"Fifth, remember to keep things active, especially in regard to boys and young men. They would rather be involved in dodgeball, basketball, biking, video games, and working on cars than they would listening to talks, doing tedious reading for homework, or visiting relatives. In previous generations, people went to concerts to sit and listen to the music. In this generation, young people want to slam-dance, sing along with the band, and jump about playing air guitar. They have a lot of nervous energy.

"And, finally, adults need to foster short-term commitments with young people. Many young people are overcommitted. They may have part-time jobs, club memberships at school, family care obligations, sports activities, homework, and girlfriends or boyfriends. Trying to get them to commit to some long-term obligation seems too confining for them. They will resist it. So, win them over a little at a time. Once they realize you are not trying to monopolize their lives and that what you want them to be involved in is of interest and of benefit to them, they will, of their own accord, provide more commitment. Try to keep in mind that, in many ways, they learned this fear of commitment by witnessing the climbing divorce rate, the ever-increasing mobility of families being transferred by companies from state to state, and by the massive layoffs brought about by company downsizing. Our generation spooked them."

What Will Today's Child Inherit?

The family of the near future will be structured differently; this we have established already in this chapter. Beyond that, however, it will look different, because the people of the future, themselves, will be different. The crossing over to a new century (and new millennium) will be the ushering in of an era populated by people who will be better educated and informed (thanks to mass media); who will live longer and enjoy better health (thanks to advances in both medicine and technology); and who will be more conscious of their place in the global society, as opposed to just in the United States (thanks to increased international commerce, the ease of buying products from other nations over the Internet, the ease of international travel, the development of a stronger world bank, and the uniting of nations in economic alliances).

At the turn of this past century, the average American lived between forty-five and fifty years. By the year 2000, most Americans will live between seventy-five and eighty years. Our society is living longer. Thanks to DNA research and biochemical engineering, by the year 2050, the average American will live to be from eighty to eighty-five years old. For most people, this sounds very promising. Unfortunately, having a nation in which the youth are outnumbered by the elderly presents some amazing financial, political, and cultural problems.

Consider this: In 1907 in America, for every five people who were over the age of sixty-five, there were fifty children under the age of eighteen. By 1997 for every five people over sixty-five, there were only seven children under age eighteen. By the year 2007, the number will be about equal, and by 2027, there will be more people over sixty-five than there will be children under eighteen.

This is significant. Why? Because it hints at a greater division than just age. Think of this: Older people are the most dependable group when it comes to getting out and voting, and by the year 2027, 50 percent of all legal voters will be over the age of fifty-five. Suppose this group of older citizens votes en masse to increase Social Security benefits, to increase Medicare and Medicaid payments, to have the federal government provide free retirement-home facilities, and to ban taxes on money withdrawn from individual retirement accounts (IRAs). Why, this would be heaven on earth for these folks, and it would all be legal and official. The problem is, the other 50 percent of the voters—those folks aged eighteen to fifty-four—would probably see this as a ridiculous financial burden for them to bear, and they might simply refuse to shoulder it.

Wouldn't that be anarchy? Indeed. But how do you suppress anarchy when the people you have hired to suppress it (the police, the military, the teachers, the ministers, the town councils) are the rebels themselves?

Already, the benefits for the elderly in this country are top-heavy. In 1996, the U.S. government's two highest domestic expenses (aside from the military and the interest on the national debt) were Medicare and Social Security. The *one year* price tag for those two systems was a staggering $552,000,000,000. (Yes, *billions!*) And who was supposed to pay for this? None other than all of the people currently employed. It's known as the put-in-pull-out plan. And it works, so long as there are more people paying in than there are people pulling out. But what happens when that is no longer the case? You either increase taxes or you reduce benefits.

"It's like a snake swallowing its own tail," says economist Mitchell Sheer of Indiana University. "You soon get a lesson in diminishing return. Either the people develop an underground economy so that they can circumvent the tax laws, or else the benefits get adjusted to reflect the reality of what cash is available. Of course, this is bound to create some hard feelings either way for the under-fifty-five crowd. If Social Security benefits are changed so that they don't start until age seventy-three or age seventy-five, these people will have to work that much longer before they will be eligible. However, if the system is kept in place as is and just goes bust, these folks won't get anything back at all for all the years they paid into the system. It's a lose-lose proposition, and many of them are already angry about what's ahead of them."

Dr. Sheer says that politicians and economists have suggested ways of dealing with this crisis, but each solution has its own new set of consequences.

"Suppose you try to solve the problem by encouraging large numbers of foreigners to immigrate to America," explains Dr. Sheer. "That would definitely make the number of young people larger than the number of elderly people. But who is to say that these immigrants would be educated, hard-working, loyal new citizens who would be eager to pay their taxes? And who is to say they wouldn't just underbid a native-born American and take his or her job away? That wouldn't be good. No . . . there is no quick fix to this problem."

According to Dr. Sheer and others who have studied this problem, the unprecedented economic prosperity that Americans experienced in the post–World War II years has made them think that the "good times" will just continue to "roll on." But, as we discovered in chapter 4 of this book, the economic waves reach a crest and then they begin to fall. Worse yet, they often create an undertow that makes the economic collapse even worse.

THE NEW MATERIALISM

Economic influences have always been major factors in the strengths or weaknesses of families. Prior to World War II, approximately 40 percent of all Americans owned a home. Just one decade after the war, by 1956, that percentage had doubled. By 1960, it has reached a level of 86 percent. Of all the homes standing in 1960, one-third had been built since the end of the war. America's gross national product (GNP) had doubled during this same period of time, and people were jumping headfirst into consumerism. Televisions, automobiles, deep freezers, bedroom suites, hi-fi's, jewelry, nice clothes, modern ranges and refrigerators, books, and records were being purchased almost as fast as they could be manufactured.

During the rise of what economists now refer to as the age of "the new materialism," a generation was raised to believe that items their parents once considered luxuries and conveniences or even extravagances were now necessities. Everyone *had* to have an automatic washer and dryer—the very idea of having to run clothes through a wringer was barbaric. Everyone *had* to have one Sof these new gizmos called a "transistor radio"—the very thought of cluttering your living room with a four-foot-tall tube radio was out of the question. Everyone *had* to have a car with an automatic transmission—the very notion of still driving an old-fashioned stick-shift tin lizzy was laughable.

The quest to accumulate material possessions was

both an economic altering of the American family's way of life *and* a drastic shift in the mind-set of people. Surveys and polls taken in the 1980s made this mind-shift graphically obvious: Of people born before 1927, only 15 percent said that their goal in life had been to get placement in "a high-paying job." However, of those persons who grew up between 1935 and 1955, 34 percent said that a high-paying job had been their top priority in life. Those persons who were born during the 1960s reported that landing a high-paying job *with bonuses and "perks"* was the chief goal in life for 56 percent of them. Similarly, people beyond age 70 reported that owning a home had been important to only 16 percent of them, whereas 43 percent of people born during and after the 1960s said that they *expected* to own "nice" homes.

Whereas economists can report on the effects of the new materialism, it falls to the sociologists to explain why it happened, and why it happened at such a breakneck speed.

"The motives were not as selfish as they seemed, at least in the beginning," says Allyn Decker, a consultant on human motivation and professor at Grace College. "Many of the men who were heading families during the 1950s had been soldiers and sailors during the war. Prior to that, they had grown up during the Great Depression. Going from poverty to combat didn't provide many happy experiences during their formative years. Thus, the common thought among men of this generation was 'Well, maybe I had to have it rough all my life, but I sure as heck am going to make sure it isn't that way for *my* kids!' And, as such, they did what they could to indulge their children.

"Of course, the problem with this was," continues Prof. Decker, "the children they reared had no memory or knowledge of either the Depression or the Second World War. As such, they assumed that having a nice home filled with nice furniture and leading a life in which all they did was go to school and play (no farm labor for this generation) was the way life was supposed to be. For everyone. So, they willingly accepted whatever was given them, demanded even more if they felt they could get away with it, and ultimately left home with a desire to exceed even the materialistic accumulations of their parents."

Prof. Decker points out an element of irony in all this.

"The postwar parents wanted to create a home in which everyone was together, and happy, and loving, and unified. However, by exposing their offspring to so many enjoyable products and material goods, they created a lust in them to obtain *things* rather than to invest time in developing relationships and enhancing family unity. What the parents considered to be 'the good life' was a traditional family unit, living in its own home, watching television together and enjoying each other's company. What the children gleaned from this was a different message, one that said there *was* no good life *unless you owned* the home, the television, and all the other material goods. Thus, they were eager to leave the family, get their own jobs (better than Dad's), and spend all their time pursuing their own efforts at materialistic accumulation."

True, there were some warnings that this was beginning to get out of hand. An occasional song, such as "Cat's in the Cradle" by Harry Chapin, which warned of a father discovering after his children were raised that he had never established a relationship with them because he had always been away at work, would raise a red flag. However, most listeners nodded and agreed that the guy had a point, but right now they were too tied up with work to do anything about it.

As the third generation came into its own, it had more time for leisure but far less time for family-oriented activities. This, of course, was because the "time together" that had been coveted by the parents of the 1950s had been changed into a desire for "time for personal pursuits" by the parents and children of the 1980s and 1990s.

And what has this individualism done to the texture of the family? For a fact, it has made it into an ever-evolving concept. How one "fits in" to bonding groups seems as important now, and for the future, as it used to be for the nuclear family.

Bob Hostetler, coauthor with Josh McDowell of *Right From Wrong* (Dallas: Word Books, 1994), explains it this way: "In the past, people defined family as a group of individuals related to each other by marriage, birth, or adoption. Today, however, a majority of adults define a family as those people one cares deeply about and all those people who care deeply about that person. Such a definition, obviously, means that the family of tomorrow may not encompass the same group that constitutes the family today. Family members may be added or subtracted according to feelings. A person may decide he or she cares for a different set of people tomorrow or next month or next year. The idea of 'family' will no longer be based on a legal definition or a biblical standard, but completely on emotions and attitudes."

Hostetler predicts that the family of the year 2000 and beyond will be both fluid and temporary, with no risks and no binding commitments. He asserts that this trend is already evident in schools, the media, and even the relationships young people have with their friends.

"My research shows that three out of five young people are already buying into this idea of what I call *'nouveau* family,'" says Hostetler. "Only thirty-two precent of teens possess a traditional perspective of what constitutes a family (birth, adoption, or marriage). To my surprise, nine percent of all teens we surveyed said they considered a family to be any group that just lived together or even merely shared the same goals. Thus, unmarried cohabiting couples and homosexual unions were automatically labeled 'families' by these teens. Whether most people would agree with them or not is a moot point; what is worth observing is the fact that their reasoning and their corresponding behavior are already set. And if they are a large segment of the next generation, their attitudes are going to impact the overall interpretation of what 'family' means."

Hostetler points out that, whereas changes once took from fifteen to thirty years really to become evident, the cycles are turning over much faster today. In one of his surveys, teens were asked certain questions in 1987, and a new group of teens was asked the same questions in 1994. Their responses related to family and home life showed noticeable changes.

Teens were asked, "Is home where you feel comfortable and would rather be than elsewhere?" In 1987, 10 percent said yes, but in 1994 only 7 percent said yes. When asked, "Is home a place where each family member is trying to love everyone," the teens of 1987 answered "yes" 11 percent of the time, but in 1994 only 9 percent of the time.

"What you see here," says Hostetler, "is that numbers that were not very encouraging to begin with are changing negatively even more rapidly than in any previous generation. Sociologists will have to determine whether this means that the previous concepts of family are no longer meeting the needs of today's Americans [something Hostetler, himself, does *not* believe] or that we are heading toward a society that is destined for more loneliness and isolation than it can imagine at present."

Counterpointing Hostetler's view that loneliness is a companion of isolation are people who never (or rarely) come in contact with other human beings in a direct sense, yet who converse and visit with dozens of people each day. These are members of the electronic-age civilization; they "reside" on the Internet and, to that end, consider their friends *and family* to be the people they interface (if not interact) with each day.

The Global Village
Gets Satellite Dishes

Perhaps one reason today's younger generation is less apt to identify with the traditional family unit is that many of them "connect" with others electronically.

"Look at it from my perspective," says a female student at Purdue University. "I was crippled in a hit-and-run accident several years ago. Because of that, certain doors have been closed to me. There's no reason for me to go to dances; I can't get involved in sports activities; my career options are limited to desk-work opportunities; and I cannot drive a car. I do have some male friends, but I'm not exactly at the top of most boys' lists for hot dates. So, to broaden my horizons, I turn to the Internet. That's one place where I can be equal to everyone else."

This young lady emphasizes the point that although people are curious to learn about others they meet on-line, there certainly is no screening process nor interview to endure.

"The people I interact with don't know if I'm Irish or Indian," says the female student. "They don't know if my skin is black, tan, or white. They don't know if I'm rich or dirt-poor. And, best of all, they don't know if I can walk or not. None of that means anything to them. All they want to know is, do I have some time to talk and to be their friend. My answer to that is, yes, yes, yes!"

Echoing these feelings is Jama Kehoe-Bigger, a forty-four-year old woman who co-owns a newsletter writing and printing business with her husband, John. They run their business out of their home in Muncie and service several clients throughout central Indiana. They are the parents of two boys in their early teens, and they lead very active lives. Jama serves as cochair of the Midwest Writers Workshop committee, which organizes a large writers' conference each July. She also writes and publishes the committee's press releases and quarterly newsletter. She even finds time to do freelance writing for a variety of specialty periodicals. What is distinctive about Mrs. Kehoe-Bigger is that she has been wheelchair-bound since before she was married.

"I had a diving accident in which I almost was killed," explains Jama. "After many years of therapy, I learned how to get out of my wheelchair and walk with special crutches, and today I can even drive a car. But my mobility is obviously very limited. However, because I deal with most of my clients on the Internet, and because I can do my writing and page layout work on the computer, most people have no idea that I am physically challenged. I prefer it that way."

Jama's autobiography, *Then Came a Miracle* (Old Tappan, New Jersey: Fleming H. Revell Co., 1982), told the story of her family's support in encouraging her to stay at her therapy and regain her strength.

"In those days, a person in my condition had no one to turn to except her parents," she recalls. "Today, it's much different. People can find support groups on-line and chat rooms at every turn. If a person has a computer and is linked to the Net, his or her range of friends is virtually limitless."

Because this is true, there have been reports of some jealousies between the traditional family members and the extended "on-line family" members. According to *The Wall Street Journal* (March 20, 1997, p. R-4), a young lady named Christy Nichols "used to get frustrated by the amount of time her mother spent on-line" with friends she would visit at a 3-D chat site.

Christy's mother, Rebecca Badger, was dying of multiple sclerosis and cancer. Wheelchair-bound, yet able to type on a computer, Rebecca adopted the name of "Robin" and spent hours each day putting words into the mouth of a cartoon character (an avatar) that represented her on screen in a three-dimensional world called "the Palace." Communicating in real time, Rebecca had her character talk with other characters who were being given lines of dialogue from other computer typists.

The Palace consisted of many rooms where "Robin" could walk and meet old friends, get introduced to new folks, read her poetry to a listening audience, or just sit as others around her "talked" about the news and events of their lives.

Rebecca's daughter, Christy, soon came to realize that this was the only means her mother had of making any contact with the outside world, so she forfeited some of her own precious remaining hours with her mother in order to let Rebecca go visiting in cyberspace. Ultimately, when Rebecca died, her friends at the Palace created a special place called "Robin's Garden," complete with giant redwood trees and a quaint cottage in the distance. Here, in this imaginary spot, they all gathered and held a memorial service for her, their on-screen characters expressing condolences, crying, reading passages from her favorite poems, and consoling one another.

Some experts believe behavior such as this proves that there is a strong need to protect and preserve the traditional family unit: If people cannot find such a relationship, they will manufacture it and role-play their part. Other experts say that this is what is so marvelous about the electronic age: Everyone can have a family, even if he or she has to go into cyberspace to locate one.

Whether they agree on its being for the better or for the worse, the one thing all experts agree on is that the family of the pre-1960s era has been altered profoundly—in makeup, in goals, in desires, in values and in codependency. Folks have gone from *Leave It to Beaver* to leave it to bytes, and from the nuclear family to the *nouveau* family.

Creating a family in the future will be a lot like creating a Web site: Click . . . design . . . then live with it.

10: Preparing for Life in the New Millennium

BY NOW you have figured out that the goal of this book has not only been to inform you of the myriad ways the world is advancing and changing, but also to help you discern ways in which you can prepare for these changes and even use them to your advantage. We have discussed economics, sports, politics, family life, technology, and numerous other influences on your life.

Now, however, in this last chapter, we are going to shift our focus. Instead of looking outward at the external factors that *try* to control your life, we are going to look inward at internal factors that you *do* have control over. By this, I am referring to attitude, enthusiasm, discipline, motivation, and drive.

If you approach the new millennium with an attitude of fear and dread, you will not be able to capitalize on all the marvelous opportunities the advances of science, technology, and education have to offer. If, on the other hand, you advance toward the year 2000 with energy, confidence, and enthusiasm, the world can be your oyster. Let's see now how this latter scenario can be yours.

The Rewards of Extra Effort

Have you ever considered how many times a day you testify to the fact that you've lost some form of competition by a very narrow margin? It doesn't matter what your area of competition is—sales, investing, athletics, contracting, elections—your losses are usually measured in very narrow margins.

Consider for a moment the many catchphrases we have to convey near misses:

"... he barely edged me out. ..."

"... we were only off by a whisker. ..."

"... if only I'd arrived one minute earlier. ..."

The list of clichés is endless because, quite frankly, so are the daily experiences of close calls. We have come to accept second place finishes as a part of life. And that's too bad, really. With just a little more effort, you could be the first-place finisher. All it takes is the extra burst of energy that comes from your own self-generated enthusiasm.

And talk about worth it! An increased effort can bring you a dramatic increase in earned rewards. Let me prove it to you.

During the 1982 Indianapolis 500 race, Gordon Johncock's car developed severe handling problems. Through a concentrated application of skill and determination, Johncock was able to overcome those mechanical difficulties and finish the race in first place, only 0.16 seconds ahead of Rick Mears. That fraction of a second, however, proved to be worth thousands of dollars. Johncock received $271,851 for winning—which was $67,700 more than Mears received for finishing second.

So it has always been in life, and will be even more so during the new millennium. That extra measure of skill, that extra effort of service, that extra investment of time always makes the difference between first place and "also ran."

But how can a willing competitor gain the confidence, knowledge, and timing needed to produce these extra advantages? And how does a person learn to make these extra advantages work in his or her favor? There are numerous techniques and systems you can use to gain a competitive advantage, some of which we will address in this chapter. But none of these plans and ideas will work to your full advantage unless you first infuse enthusiasm into each one.

THE KEY WORD IS ENTHUSIASM

In all forms of competition, the key word is enthusiasm. Enthusiasm will help you visualize your future success in concrete terms and show you how to go after it. It will provide powerful physical energy, incredible mental activity, and amazing overall stamina. It will give you a positive view of life. And, best of all, it will make you eager to enter the new millennium rather than shy away from its changes and challenges.

If you've never been a person who becomes easily enthused about things, it may be because you've felt bashful or reserved or unsure of your ability to make good, later on, of any earlier displays of enthusiasm.

For most people, it is not very difficult to generate a temporary feeling of enthusiasm. But temporary, short-lived enthusiasm is of no competitive value to you. It will only be from *sustained* enthusiasm that you will be able to stay loyal to a regimen of "progress through work." Persistence and endurance pay off in any situation, whether you are trying to build muscles or develop an on-line consulting business.

Why is it that many people have no enthusiasm about entering the next millennium? Why does a person lose his or her enthusiasm under any circumstances, new millennium or not? Why do some people "throw in the towel" halfway through something?

Oddly enough, I don't believe the answer can be attributed to fear, weakness, boredom, or frustration, although these symptoms, too, will eventually manifest themselves. I think the chief cause is *blurred vision*—the inability to maintain a clear vision of one's goals and rewards.

We must believe that we are capable of reaching our goals in the next millennium. In order to develop such faith, we may need to enhance our education, improve our current reputation, or spend some time building our self-confidence. Then, once we see that we are capable of achieving our goals, our nervousness and anxiety will start to fade, and we will see our goals clearly.

We must maintain our enthusiasm to remain on course. Our persistence, even during the darkest situations, will see us through to the attainment of our goals. We must know how to maintain our courage, keep faith in ourselves, and stay on track. And through it all, our extra edge and secret advantage will come from our sustained enthusiasm.

You already possess enough excitement about life, energy for work, and determination of spirit to maintain enthusiasm about everything you do. You proved that when you picked up this book and spent time reading the first nine chapters. Your curiosity about life around you and about coming events shows that you have an internal drive and power that can make you a winner. All you need to do is tap those positive sources.

THE POWER OF BELIEF

Have you ever stopped to think that being average means that you are as close to the bottom as you are to the top? You're neither a winner nor a loser.

The motivated, enthusiastic person has a strong desire to become someone special in the next millennium. This person uses his or her mind to develop plans for personal development. Learning to maximize the use of one's mind is the foundation for self-advancement. It is something you can do, starting now.

It has been said that ideas are a dime a dozen, but the people who use them are priceless. A corollary to that statement should be that people who know how to stimulate ideas are even further ahead of the game. In coming years, a person's ability to think clearly and logically, to concentrate, to make decisions, and to research ideas will enable that person to tackle any problem or obstacle before him or her. A person must "think success" before he or she can *achieve* success.

Now-classic studies conducted more than four decades ago by Dr. Maxwell Maltz revealed the importance of the human mind in regard to success and motivation. The human mind has a powerful element that the minds of lesser beings do not possess: an *imagination.* With it, people can become creators of art, poetry, dance, machinery, corporate structures, and business strategies.

Maltz's psycho-cybernetic studies revealed that man's central nervous system is incapable of distinguishing between real and imagined situations. For example, if a man dreams that he is being chased by a bear, he will begin to breathe faster, his heart will start to race, and his forehead will begin to bead with perspiration, just as if the event were real. A nightmare can often be a very terrifyingly "real" event.

Maltz noted, however, that the imagination could also be used for positive image-building. If the mind could vicariously experience a successful speech or a successful sale or a successful trip to the batter's box, and if the mind could replay this particular scene of success often enough, it would become as convincingly real from a positive perspective as the nightmare had been from a negative perspective.

It is by conscious, rational thought that our subconscious thoughts and reactions can be changed. Our decisions, actions, and emotions are reactions to our beliefs. Whatever our minds believe to be true *will* be true to the rest of our bodily functions. Hence, if our minds tell us that we are great orators, we will remain calm and in control when we appear before a crowd. Conversely, if our minds tell us that we are poor orators, we will experience racing hearts, moist palms and foreheads, and stammering speech. Truth is what we perceive truth to be. Thus, if we begin to think now that the future has nothing but positive options for us, once the year 2000 arrives, we will be set to take advantage of those options.

Mental practice will make perfect. It is not arrogance or egotism to imagine ourselves in a success mode. Too many of us degrade and underrate our abilities to the point that our emphasized humility leads us to feelings of inadequacy. Failure soon follows. It is far better to program ourselves to think of being successes in the coming years.

The mental programming for success that we need to undertake can be thought of as *serious make-believe*. It is like the make-believe games we used to play as children, in which we pictured ourselves as knights, cowboys, nurses, fashion models, soldiers, or school teachers. This time, however, the game is for real. This time, when we imagine ourselves as millionaires, athletic champions, valedictorians, top salespeople, or company presidents, we will not later erase the image.

Our images of ourselves as successes in the new millennium is not something we can be nonchalant about; we must treat it seriously. Rather than daydream from time to time, we should visualize ourselves in whatever role we desire our future to hold for us. We should consider such things as what we will wear, what we will say, and what we will be in control of. The more precise we can be in our visualizations, the more real these roles will become to us. The more real they become, the faster we will be drawn to them. Positive thoughts produce positive results. If you act like a success, others will perceive you as a success. Envision only victory. Remember that success attracts success.

If you are optimistic, you will find yourself able to

cope with virtually any situation. From John Milton's *Paradise Lost* comes the adage, "The mind is its own place, and in itself can make a Heav'n of Hell, a Hell of Heav'n." Abraham Lincoln stated it more simply when he once wrote, "Most people are about as happy as they make up their minds to be."

How can we be happy? By putting our minds at ease about what is ahead for us in the year 2000 and beyond. How can this be done? Through common-sense behavior: not worrying about things you cannot control; reacting calmly and levelheadedly during times of crisis; feeling and acting happy; treating other people warmly; and behaving as though your future success is inevitable.

CONFRONTING AND CONTROLLING ANXIETY ABOUT THE FUTURE

Anxiety is one of the greatest elements in undermining enthusiasm. You cannot behave like a highly motivated individual if you are burdened with guilt, fear, confusion, or tension. You can come to grips with feelings of anxiety only by confronting them. Here are starting points:

- After an honest evaluation of a negative situation, decide if there is really any logical reason for your distress.
- If your anxiety is exaggerated, put it into its proper perspective or forget it completely.
- If your anxiety is legitimate, remind yourself that you can find a solution to your problem if you stay calm and use your creative problem-solving talents.

Probably nothing will serve you better in overcoming negative mental attitudes than the ability to believe in yourself and your capabilities. If you can foster this self-confidence, you can do almost anything.

Belief is vital. Many years ago, I learned a simple but powerful lesson about the power of belief. The simple event that taught me this lesson has had an ongoing impact on my life. It taught me that I must have complete confidence in myself if I am to succeed at whatever I set out to do.

At the time, my youngest brother-in-law, Tim, was still in high school and living with his parents. One day, when my wife and I were visiting, Tim and I happened to be watching television together. A talk show guest was showing the audience how to juggle. While Tim watched and listened intently, and ran to find three tennis balls to practice with, I grew bored with it all.

When the show ended, Tim attempted to follow the juggler's instructions. He even made me stand up and try it a few times. The tennis balls bounced around the living room, I felt foolish, and Tim—arms flailing in the air—looked silly to me.

"Forget it," I said. "That stuff's for circus performers. Guys like us are too old to master something like that. You probably have to start practicing when you're a kid."

Undaunted, Tim went off to his bedroom to continue his practicing. During the rest of our visit, I laughed every time I heard the tennis balls bouncing off walls and furniture.

About two weeks later, Tim came to see my wife and me. He brought along three tennis balls.

"Look at this," he said proudly. He tossed the tennis balls into the air and juggled them for five full rotations before dropping them. "Not bad, eh? I'm really getting better. A little more practice, and I'll have it down pat."

I was stunned. He could actually do it. I had told him it was impossible, but he had believed it *was* possible. And his belief had *made* it possible. He had mastered juggling.

Suddenly, something occurred to me: If this gangly high school kid could learn to juggle, I knew good and well that I could, too . . . if I set my mind to it. I was not about to let some awkward young kid show me up. I promised myself that I would learn to juggle or die trying. It became an obsession with me. I bought tennis balls and practiced every day. At night, as I lay in bed, I would mentally rehearse the movements—the timing, the pitches, and the catches.

A week later, I could do two full rotations. In two weeks, I could juggle for three minutes before dropping the balls. In three weeks, I could juggle as long as I wanted to keep going. In one month's time, I had gone from thinking I could never learn to juggle in a simple cascade motion to mastering it, and an over-the-top cascade, and even a forehand forward-grab rotation.

What caused this advancement? Two things: *motivation* (I just couldn't let my little brother-in-law show me up) and *belief* (the knowledge that if Tim could learn to juggle, so could I).

Since then, whenever I am confronted by a task that seems impossible, I remember the juggling episode. I remind myself of the power I have within to conquer anything, so long as I believe in myself, maintain an earnest concentration on the problem, and devote time every day to meeting the challenge. As I noted earlier, mental practice does make perfect. Along with that, belief is indispensable.

BELIEF AND MOTIVATION

It is impossible to separate belief from motivation. One cannot have a driving belief in something without being motivated by that belief. Similarly, one cannot be greatly motivated without believing in something. But what are the elements that can create a belief, a confidence in ourselves? In my experience, several of those elements have been as follows:

1. *A Clear Conscience.* You must feel that what you are about to engage in is within the ethical, moral, professional, and social codes of your personal convictions, and that the job you undertake will measure up to your personal standards of honesty, fairness, and trust. If the work does not meet these criteria, you will find yourself resisting it and struggling against it.

2. *Adequate Knowledge.* You must feel that you either have, or will be able to obtain, the needed instructions, training, and experience to handle the task at hand. If you feel that you are inadequately prepared for the work, you will be hesitant in your actions, slow with your decisions, and overly cautious with your recommendations.

3. *A Worthwhile Mission.* You must be convinced that the task you are about to accept is a worthy job, in the sense that it will make some sort of positive contribution to yourself, your family, or your business, or to society. More than likely, you will not be motivated by salary alone. We all need to feel that our lives are being used for something worthwhile.

4. *Potential Advancement.* You must be convinced that once you complete the job or master the skill, you will be better off because of it. If the successful completion of your goal does not reward you with a social, economic, or personal prize, you will be hard-pressed to justify why you should be involved in it.

If your situation encompasses the above four elements, your belief will be strong in whatever you attempt to do. This belief will drive you forward to success. People with confidence and belief are motivated and eager to face challenges, both now and in the next millennium. They have boundless energy. They are life's positive workaholics, the leaders who have the mental stability and creativity to push their businesses or communities or art forms to the top. And you now know how to formulate the same positive mental image of yourself as they do of themselves. There is no reason you cannot have the same level of success that they enjoy. Go for it. Starting a new millennium is like beginning life with a clean slate: All mistakes are erased.

ENTHUSIASM AND DECISION MAKING

I said earlier that enthusiasm makes the difference between just doing a job and doing a job well. But no amount of enthusiasm or motivation can make up for a lack of skills and discipline. In fact, the full potential of enthusiasm can be realized only when it is applied to mastering the activities required by the work you do.

Thomas Wolfe wrote, "If a man has talent and cannot use it, he has failed. If he has a talent and uses only half of it, he has partly failed. If he has a talent and learns somehow to use the whole of it, he has gloriously succeeded, and won a satisfaction and a triumph few men ever know." It is through enthusiasm that you will learn how to use the whole of your talent and your skills and, thus, win the success you desire.

Famed psychologist William James advised, "Believe that life is worth living, and your belief will help create the fact."

Belief begins in the mind. Enthusiasm and motivation are stimulated by confidence and belief in one's mission in life. Once having mastered the ability to envision yourself as a dynamic leader, you must also learn how to use the powers of your mind for a variety of positive activities. One of the first is the act of making decisions.

One of the most challenging mental tasks any of us will have to face during the next millennium will be making tough decisions. The process will become even more agonizing if the fate of other people (our family members, our friends, our employees) rides on our choices and rulings. The anxiety can often be so unbearable, many people refuse to make a decision at all. Of course, choosing not to decide is, itself, a decision. (And, I might add, a very poor one.)

There are many leaders who claim to thrive on decision making. It makes them feel powerful and in control. These positive feelings remain as long as the decisions are solid and wise. However, not all decisions are.

Snap decisions are reflex actions and should be avoided. The full consequences of hastily determined conclusions are usually not realized until it is too late to reverse them.

Alternative decisions—choosing among several possible courses of action—need to be faced, whether bad or good. For example, you may one day be faced with a decision as to whether you should sell one of your factories or fire thirty-five of your senior employees. It's a no-win situation, but if you ignore it, you will eventually lose both the factory *and* the workers. So, a decision must be made at the time of crisis.

Successful decision makers are people who seek to reach a decision which will be most beneficial for themselves and for the people upon whom the decision will impact. They know that there are only two possible answers to the decision at hand: yes and no. Conversely, there is a limitless range of questions that could have a bearing on the decision. Successful decision makers seek the appropriate questions. They consult their friends, coworkers, colleagues, managers, and other experts in the field. From them, they acquire a variety of viewpoints, which ultimately lead to questions such as these:

1. Will we need additional personnel or training?
2. To keep pace with modern advances, what will we need in the way of equipment, storage space, and inventory?
3. How will we handle advertising, marketing, and distribution?
4. What about returns, breakage, insurance, quantity discounts, and delivery?
5. How will we handle financing, bookkeeping, and pricing?
6. Who are our competitors and what are they offering?

Having obtained a list of questions from a wide variety of people, you must next sort out which questions are specifically applicable to the current decision. Keep yourself open to questions, ideas, and information that may be contrary to your own feelings and opinions. Your objective will be to become aware of the total picture, knowing full well that the further we advance into the future, the more complex many situations will become. Since the ramifications of your decision may affect many people and last a long time, you will need to be open to all views and perspectives, even if you later opt to reject some.

As you focus on answering the questions, you will mentally be making check marks on the pro and con sides of the decision. After a period of summary reflection, you will be able to make your decision in view of which side is most heavily weighted. Of course, one's "gut instinct" or "intuition" will at times be worth heeding, too. But, generally speaking, logic and factual analysis regarding important decision making will be your best bets.

CONCENTRATION

Ralph Waldo Emerson noted that "Concentration is the secret of success in politics, in war, in trade; in short, in *all* the management of human affairs."

The ability to concentrate intently on a matter will remain one of the key aspects of personal motivation as we enter the new millennium. The person who can concentrate on a project will also be capable of contemplating its successful completion. And anyone who can "see" victory ahead will be eager to pursue the mark.

Concentration is a valuable mental skill that should be cultivated by all success-seeking people. Intense concentration is an acquired talent. We all have the power to concentrate. More importantly, we all have the ability greatly to enhance this capability.

The ability to lose oneself in deep concentration is a skill few people ever fully master. Those who do are seldom understood by others. According to popular legend, when Albert Einstein was developing his most advanced mathematical equations and theories, he often dressed in a most bizarre fashion, wearing socks of different colors, a sweater vest atop a pullover sweater, and tennis shoes with a dress coat. It wasn't that he purposely desired to look eccentric; his thoughts were so deeply focused on his work that he had "no thoughts" for routine matters.

Einstein's accomplishments were incredible. Nevertheless, the world would be in chaos if everyone was lost in intense concentration on just one topic the way Einstein was. What will be of more value to you will be the ability to turn on an intensity of concentration whenever it will be needed to solve problems, to adapt to the future's changing environment, to develop new ideas, and to formulate game-plan strategies.

There may be any number of reasons why you may not have already developed good concentration habits. You may have had to contend with noise, visual distractions, or stress. I have found that it is best to deal with disruptive matters in direct ways:

- For *noise*: close your door; disconnect your phone or have your calls held; ask people to contact you by E-mail; create "white noise" with an FM radio, a humming fan, or a dehumidifier; use earplugs; work at the library.
- For *clutter*: work on a cleared desk; focus on one task at a time; remove family pictures or anything that might cause you to daydream; open one folder at a time, as needed; store as much in your computer as possible so as to eliminate many files and folders.
- For *interruption control*: use and enforce "Do Not Disturb" signs; schedule private time each day; assemble all of your supplies in advance so that you don't keep getting up from your desk to sharpen a pencil, refill a coffee cup, retrieve a book or locate some files.

Concentration is enhanced in a variety of ways. The more factors you are able to have working in your favor, the greater the odds that your concentration will be improved. Strive for:

1. A quiet environment
2. Advance organization of time and materials
3. Belief in the job at hand
4. Proper frame of mind
5. Determination and perseverance
6. Anticipation of current challenge
7. Confidence in yourself
8. Suitable reward for completing the job
9. Curiosity about new approaches to old problems

As we have already noted, your mind is your greatest asset in business, society, and self-fulfillment. The more you can discipline your mind to concentrate on solving problems and meeting the challenges of the coming new era, the more you will be able to capitalize on the corresponding opportunities.

CREATIVE "RIGHTERS"

Once you have improved your concentration techniques, your next challenge will be to go beyond mere problem solving. The twenty-first century will be a time of great advances. To be a part of this advancement, you will have to take your way of thinking to the next level: the conceptualization of creativity. It will be from your mind that the new products, new services, and new operating procedures will be drawn. Let me show you ways to initiate these processes.

I teach dozens of writing seminars each year. Many of my students say, "I don't know how creative writers do it. Time and again, they come up with new plots, new characters, and even new ways to use the language. They must be gifted."

If these people could have seen the pile of rejection letters I accumulated during the years I was first struggling to get published, they would realize that a creative "gift" takes a long time to develop. Most creative writers will admit that they are not gifted. They are simply people who have, through years of practice, learned how to stimulate creativity.

I'm convinced the same talent has been developed in many people who are obvious leaders. But these people display their talents as creative *righters*, rather than *writers*. Whenever something goes wrong—an illness in the family, a sales decline at the company, a crisis in the community—and a solution is needed to set things right, the creative righters are always the ones called upon to handle the situation.

Creative righters know how to play with symbols, ideas, names, and numbers to produce a fresh concept. Whereas no one can create something out of a void, it is also true that the reservoir of stored experiences locked in our memories can be forced to the surface to give us current perspectives on the task at hand.

We have a wealth of experiences—the books we've read, the television shows and movies we've watched, the conversations we've had, the places we've visited, and the jobs we've held. If all of this can be tapped, there is no end to the new concepts that can be formulated. Creative righters know how to go about tapping these resources. Here are some procedures you can borrow from them:

Go against the grain. All successful creative thinkers dare to buck tradition. They contemplate radical thoughts. Copernicus asked, "But what if the earth *isn't* the center of the universe?" Columbus wondered, "But what if the earth *isn't* flat?" More recently, other thinkers have dared to consider such outrageous possibilities as establishing colonies in space, linking all homes and businesses via the Internet, and inventing automobiles that drive themselves. Just because no one has previously conceived such an idea does not mean it isn't feasible. Daring to ask the nontraditional question leads the thinker to the next step: discovering how to make the impossible, possible. This leads to new areas of investigation and even more new questions. And that's creativity.

Don't fear mistakes. The only people who never make mistakes are the people who never try anything. Thomas Edison once noted that he "failed my way to success." He experimented with many different ways to solve a problem or make a new product work. By keeping at it until, as he put it, he "ran out of mistakes," he eventually found the solution.

I believe that all successful creative thinkers have this same attitude. They are so enthusiastic about finding an answer, they aren't thrown off by temporary setbacks. In fact, for many of them, trial and error is the most enjoyable part of the creative process.

Mix apples and oranges. Creative thinkers are nosy.

They are always snooping into other people's professions to see what they can adapt to their own. They try other jobs, read books in professional fields other than their own, attend seminars on offbeat subjects, and strike up conversations with experts in numerous professions. Many times, creative thinkers discover an innovation in one field that can be modified slightly to solve a problem in a different area.

Creative borrowing has been going on for ages. Automobile safety experts borrowed seatbelts and shatterproof glass from aviation experts. Prefabricated home builders borrowed the concept of interlocking house sections from the assembly line procedure at automobile plants. Truly creative thinkers put no blinders on their research.

Brainstorm the illogical. With no limitations or fetters on his or her thinking, the creative person looks at existing practices and tries to imagine how they might be changed. Sometimes the immediate ideas seem illogical, but the creative thinker considers them anyway. For example, the obvious logic regarding air travel in the days of the Wright Brothers was that a flying apparatus had to be lighter than air, such as a hot-air balloon. The Wrights, however, created a heavier-than-air apparatus that used torque and thrust to keep it aloft. It was illogical for the times—but, when it worked, the logic was changed.

Believe in your creative capabilities. Creative righters trust their imaginations and analytical talents. They don't give up before they get started. They know that the mind combines conscious study and subconscious analysis in the process of developing new concepts. This process takes time. Just as a computer is given data, then allowed time to search its memory banks for answers, the brain needs time to search for its references and formulate logical responses. Have faith in yourself. You can be just as creative as anyone else if you'll just take the time to explore all your thought processes.

EMOTIONAL CONTROL: RESPOND, DON'T REACT

In interviewing people from all walks of life as part of the research for this book, I discovered that a segment of society has feelings of dread or anxiety about entering a new millennium. When asked why they feel this way, their responses were ambiguous, yet real: "I can't put my finger on it exactly, but I have this sense that the year two thousand represents the start of a new way of life that I'm just not going to be ready for" . . . "I'm nervous about what the future holds because I don't feel I'm keeping pace right now" . . . "There seems to be much more bad news on television than good these days, so I worry constantly that the future may be even worse" . . . "Somehow, going into the twenty-first century seems like a tangible act rather than a figurative act—as though I will be entering a totally new world that will be alien to me and will make me isolated and scared."

Let's face it, these people are expressing what many others have given at least passing thoughts to. Any time a society makes a significant change of any sort, the disruption in "the routine" causes emotional problems for some people.

Back during the Depression, President Roosevelt kept a firm hand on the potential hysteria of the country by warning the people: "We have nothing to fear but fear itself." That's not a bad way of looking at our approach to the new millennium.

Roosevelt had endured every form of personal disappointment imaginable—from unsuccessful election campaigns to a crippling attack of polio—and had learned that brooding and worrying accomplished nothing. Victory in politics, business, and war went to those who were able to remain calm and clearheaded. Panic was the worst form of weakness. Emotional control led to rational thinking, and rational thinking led to victory.

Those same rules apply to anyone feeling tension

over the beginning of a new millennium. The woman or man who can remain steady during a time of change will always survive and do well. Better yet, the person who can remain in control when situations start to turn against her or him will be the person upon whom others will rely when the next crisis arises.

Because successful people must, by necessity these days, make procedural changes, initiate new systems, and break new ground, they quite often are open to criticism from people who do not understand the whole picture.

"Why can't she just leave well enough alone?" someone will complain.

"Who does that hot shot think he is, trying to tell *me* how to become more productive!"

"*What?* A change in our work systems. I hate this! I won't go along with it!"

Such complaints from employees, colleagues, co-workers, clients, customers, patients, and even friends can bring out the worst in people, unless they have learned how to control their emotional reactions. Successful people respond to situations; they don't react to criticism.

The most potentially dangerous of all emotions is anger. There are times when anger can be an appropriate response. Society, for example, has a right to be angered by vandalism, drunk driving, and corruption in politics. This anger is expressed and vented rationally, however, through legislation and the appointment of public officials to oversee the legal process. These are examples of emotional control at its finest level.

Our control over individual bouts of anger is usually less disciplined. Quite frankly, we don't like people to cross us. When they do, our instinctive reaction is to "get even."

People deal with anger in a variety of ways—some positive, some negative. I do not need to spend time explaining why reactions such as screaming, making threats, giving someone the silent treatment, or passively accepting all blame for an incident are negative ways of dealing with anger. Instead, let's focus on ways of coping with anger.

First, there is what I call *vicarious viciousness*. This involves venting your anger in ways other than attacking the person or circumstances you are angry with. For example, if you are angry at yourself for some mistake you have made, it would probably help if you went out in your yard and kicked a football several times. Vigorous physical activity is exceptional for diminishing anger.

Abraham Lincoln had many political enemies who did their best to thwart his plans to abolish slavery, preserve the union, and increase overseas trade. Lincoln had to work with these bullheaded people, cajoling and persuading until he obtained their cooperation. As an outlet for the anger he frequently experienced, Lincoln made it a practice to sit down and write very harsh letters to these people, in which he insulted, ridiculed, and even threatened them. Then he would burn the letters. Just venting his anger in this vicarious way helped him stay in control of his emotions.

A second way to handle anger is by *rerouting* it. If, for example, your pet project collapses, immediately turn your frustration and anger to a new project. "I can't believe my partners wouldn't go along with the idea of expanding our Web sites so that every aspect of our company could be showcased. All right, then, I'll just have to maximize the use of the one Web site we do have as a way of proving how valuable they can be. *That's* my new goal!"

A third way to handle anger is through *courteous confrontation*. This requires you to control your temper but insist that your rights not be violated. "I appreciate the problems you've had with bad weather and slow delivery dates for materials, Mr. Williams, but according to the contract we signed, you agreed to build my new garage for sixty-five hundred dollars. That's the amount I will be paying. Cost overruns are your responsibility, I'm afraid."

Controlling anger is something we all must work at diligently. If you become angry more easily than most people, admit it and do something about it. You might begin by carrying a notebook with you for a week. Jot down those things that cause you to become angry. Correct the minor ones: "Marie, you've been late every morning this week. Please try to arrive no later than 8:00 a.m. from now on." Diffuse the major ones: Schedule a handball game for immediately after a meeting with your most irksome client.

Anger is a natural human response to negative circumstances. By channeling its unleashed powers in positive directions, not only can you control it, you can also make it useful.

BATTLING THE BLAHS

Back during the 1960s, an old man was asked, "What do you think of all these miniskirts?" The old man shook his head and responded, "Give people cheesecake at every meal, and eventually they'll start screaming for cornbread."

Even though in the chapters of this book we have discovered the many fascinating innovations the future will hold for us, *anything* can become routine, mundane, dull, and boring if a person has to deal with it for an extended length of time. When the novelty or challenge of an item, event, or situation wears off, boredom sets in. Boredom as a persistent emotional condition can lead to severe depression, lack of productivity, and sometimes even such radical responses as drug dependence, divorce, or suicide. Chronic boredom should not be ignored or treated lightly.

We all must contend with occasional cases of temporary boredom: a lecture we are required to attend, a "conversationalist" who buttonholes us at a party, a movie our spouse has wanted to see. Boring situations are a part of life. They are unavoidable, so we resign ourselves to them, endure them temporarily, and then seize our opportunity to escape as soon as possible.

Chronic boredom, however, provides no escape. It stays with its victim around the clock. It smothers enthusiasm, stifles imagination, and saps personal energy. In a futuristic age in which machines will be doing more of the manual labor and deep thinking for us, this will become an even greater potential threat.

People generally strive to create stability in their lives. There's nothing wrong with stability so long as it does not result in tedium. For example, stability is having a job to go to. Tedium is going to that job at the same time, by the same route 240 times per year, and then sitting at the same desk in front of the same computer, inputting the same kind of data day after day. Ho-hum. (This was why, after the energy crisis of 1979 had abated, many people continued to go to work in car pools. They had discovered that riding in different cars and having morning discussions provided a nice change of pace.)

Chronic boredom can have many serious effects on a person's life:

- Instead of being participants, bored people become spectators.
- Rather than risk failing at something, bored people make excuses for not becoming involved in new projects.
- Instead of striving to reach goals, the bored person gives up.
- Instead of cooperating, the bored person criticizes, argues with, avoids, and resents all colleagues.

In order to avoid boredom and stay motivated up to and beyond the year 2000, you must provide a more stimulating and fascinating life for yourself. Consider these suggestions:

Always be involved in some form of study. Learning new things keeps the mind agile and stimulates creativity. So, register for a seminar on Chinese cooking, sign up for a correspondence course in creative writing, listen to books on tape that teach you to speak Russian, go to the library and check out a book on time management, visit Web sites that offer advice on gardening, or join an on-line chat room that debates politics. Continually challenge your mind to grow.

Regularly take calculated risks. Break out of your comfort zone by setting your goals a little higher than usual, by promising delivery dates a little earlier than is routine, or by moving into a new social arena you haven't explored before. Don't allow yourself to become casual about life or business. Complacency can be numbing.

Try a change-of-pace activity. Attend a weekend film festival, try go-carting, experiment with virtual reality, tour a doll museum, eat at an East Indian restaurant, or visit a wildlife preserve. There's a fascinating world out there waiting to be discovered, and the access to it will only be made easier by the technology of the twenty-first century.

Keep physically fit. If you are coping with boredom (or anxiety) by snacking, then substitute games or exercise for food.

Change your appearance. Why not? Try a new hairstyle. Shave your mustache and see if anyone notices. You can try a little variety; you're not cast in steel.

Schedule a private pep rally. Try to arrange a free hour a few times each week so that you can listen to motivational tapes or view motivational video presentations on your VCR or CD-ROM. Not only will you learn some new and important life skills, you'll also rekindle your competitive fires.

Boredom, like failure, is self-inflicted. It is an avoidable emotional state. The enthusiastic, positive-thinking person *will* avoid it.

OVERCOMING SHYNESS

If one of the reasons you may be dreading the arrival of a new century, a new millennium, a new era, is because you cannot envision yourself as someone who will boldly step forward and take command of the situation, don't feel as though you are alone. In a survey conducted recently by the R & R Newkirk Company, it was reported that some eighty-five million Americans admit to being shy.

Shyness is not limited to small children who peer out from behind their mothers' skirts or to frail-looking wallflowers who sit, eyes lowered, on the sidelines at dances. Even very famous people suffer from it. Barbara Walters claims she is very uncomfortable speaking with strangers when off-camera without notes. Singer Johnny Mathis claims that in more than thirty years as an entertainer, he still hasn't overcome stage fright. If such successful people can suffer from shyness, is it any wonder that the average person is even more susceptible?

"Everyone is a potential victim of shyness," claims Dr. L. Stanley Wenck, educational psychologist at Ball State University and a contributing writer for *Essence* magazine, "because shyness is self-induced. People become shy because they lose perspective. They begin to think that everyone else is focusing on them. That's not so. The simple fact is, most people don't have the time it takes to scrutinize other people. Shy people are exaggerating their conditions."

Nevertheless, shy people find it hard to overcome their self-consciousness. That is why many of them embrace such technology as E-mail and on-line chat rooms, which allow them to communicate, yet stay hidden.

Part of the problem has been that shyness has never been considered a serious problem. Parents particularly have given it minimal consideration. "Little girls are supposed to be coy," they will say, or "The kid'll come out of his shell when he gets a little older."

But shy children often grow up to become shy adults. Shyness is not a condition that one outgrows or sheds without help.

"Shy people have specific mental traits," explains Dr. Wenck. "They analyze everything they do and usually are overly critical about themselves. They feel anxiety over how they look, walk, dress, speak, and behave. They truly desire to make the best possible impression on people but usually feel they have not succeeded."

Dr. Wenck notes that the more intense a situation is, the more intense the corresponding feeling of shyness will be. This is because shyness is nothing more than a disguise for a deeper problem: *fear*. The heart of the matter is that shy people are frightened. And since most of us have something that frightens us, we are all susceptible to shyness.

Anxiety Is Fear

Think about the last time you were scared. Remember your physical reactions? Your heart started to pound, your palms grew moist, your mouth felt like cotton, and your knees grew weak.

Now, compare those reactions to the way you felt the last time you were shy or nervous. You experienced virtually the same responses, didn't you? You had the same heart pounding, same dry mouth, same weak knees.

Shyness is most often a fear of other people. This is particularly true when those other people are strangers, authority figures, or members of the opposite sex. Rather than deal with such encounters, shy people prefer to stay home. They turn down invitations to social events and limit outside contact as much as possible.

Because shy people are so self-conscious, they fail

to mingle well with others (except possibly in cyberspace). Even when forced to engage in conversations, shy people will avoid eye contact and show little in the way of facial expressions. On a business level, some people become so tongue-tied and frustrated, they cannot do their jobs well. This is not a new phenomenon. More than four thousand years ago, the Bible reports, Moses was so awkward and shy in front of Pharaoh that he had to have his brother Aaron speak for him.

Unfortunately, we can't all have someone like Aaron do our talking for us. That's why it's important to come to grips with the problem of shyness.

How do people find the courage to overcome their sensitivity and, thus, avoid shyness? How do they gain the perspective that enables them to be self-confident rather than self-conscious? The answer lies in their ability to believe in themselves.

Some people gain this belief as the result of counseling by a teacher, minister, rabbi, or doctor. Some gain it by reading self-help books and articles. For other people, it comes as a result of someone else's faith in them. Such was the case of Dr. Audrey Sharpe, a woman who not only came to grips with her own shyness but was also able, later, to help others with the same problem.

Dr. Sharpe, an elementary school principal and educational counselor in the Fort Wayne, Indiana, public school system, is a wife, mother, doctor of educational psychology, and successful businesswoman. Yet, as a child, she had to contend with serious bouts of shyness.

"Being black, female, and overweight as a youngster, I felt very self-conscious," Dr. Sharpe recalls. "It was as though I was a member of three minority groups all at the same time. My self-worth problems became even more compounded when my mother and father separated, and my mother moved to a distant city."

For many years, Audrey maintained contact with

her mother by mail. During her youth, she lived for a while with her father, then with an aunt, and, finally, by the time she was in high school, back with her mother again.

"I felt comfortable around my brothers and sisters and was even bossy toward them at times," says Audrey, "but I was never very assertive outside the home. I loved to read and did a lot of it. I was a serious and hard-working student, too. I could hide myself in my books and try to cope with my personal feelings by myself."

Audrey's older brother and sister went to work in a poultry slaughter barn as soon as they were old enough. The work was low-paying, strenuous, smelly, and tedious. Audrey dreaded the day when she, too, would have to start working there. But being too shy to challenge the way of life that had apparently been chosen for her, she resigned herself to her fate. Then something happened to change all that.

"I was attending an all-black high school in a southern state," Audrey remembers, "and halfway through my senior year, my English teacher asked me which college I was going to attend. I told her my counselor had informed me that I was meant for manual labor, like my older brother and sister. When my English teacher heard that, she was outraged. She took me by the arm and marched me right down to that counselor. Even though the counselor was black, she accused him of being prejudiced. She demanded that I be given the precollege admission tests."

Audrey did so well on the tests, she won a scholarship to a private college. In addition, her English teacher helped her find a summer job, so that she could earn money for clothes and other things she needed for college.

"I was greatly touched by how much faith my teacher had in me," says Audrey. "I felt I just couldn't let her down. I had to do well. Her confidence in me helped me gradually develop confidence in myself. Each time I felt hesitant or shy, I thought of how boldly my teacher had marched me into that counselor's office and defended my right to a proper education. I reasoned that if she felt so positively about me, I should, too. It encouraged me and made me stronger."

Audrey is quick to add that her bout with shyness did not end after this one episode. However, with additional encouragement from her mother and, later, her husband and daughter, she grew more and more confident.

"Today, as an educator, I do my best to encourage students to be outgoing and social," notes Dr. Audrey Sharpe. "I also try to help parents be more at ease with their youngsters. Overcoming shyness is a continual challenge for many people, myself included. We all have a degree of caution built into us, and that's not all bad. The main thing is not to let it hamper us socially or academically."

OVERVIEW

Human emotions, we have discovered in this chapter, range from fear to bravery, from shyness to anger, from terror to annoyance. Emotions can and should be disciplined and channeled. As we look to the next millennium, the overwhelming discoveries we have summarized in the preceding nine chapters can appear ominous. From an emotional perspective, these discoveries and advances can be somewhat frightening, tumultuous, even threatening. Put into their proper perspective, however, they can be inspiring, exciting, and adventurous.

The amazing world of the new millennium will be what you decide to make of it. The opportunities will be limitless. The strides forward will be breathtaking. The adjustments will be challenging.

It has been the purpose of this book to show you where humankind has been, where it currently is, and where it appears to be headed. In light of that, this book has also tried to help you envision ways in which you will fit into the newest endeavors of humankind, and to provide you with lessons, information, and suggestions on how you can capitalize on the changes ahead.

Armed with insights, buoyed by confidence, directed by shared wisdom, and motivated by enthusiasm, you now have all you need to be ready as *Millennium Approaches*.

THE NATIONWIDE #1 BESTSELLER

the Relaxation Response

by Herbert Benson, M.D.
with Miriam Z. Klipper

A SIMPLE MEDITATIVE TECHNIQUE THAT HAS HELPED MILLIONS TO COPE WITH FATIGUE, ANXIETY AND STRESS

Available Now—
00676-6/ $6.99 US/ $8.99 Can

COMPREHENSIVE, AUTHORITATIVE REFERENCE WORKS FROM AVON TRADE BOOKS

THE OXFORD AMERICAN DICTIONARY
Edited by Stuart Berg Flexner, Eugene Ehrlich and
Gordon Carruth   51052-9/ $12.50 US/ $16.50 Can

THE CONCISE COLUMBIA DICTIONARY OF QUOTATIONS
Robert Andrews   70932-5/ $12.50 US/ $16.00 Can

THE CONCISE COLUMBIA ENCYCLOPEDIA
Edited by Judith S. Levey and Agnes Greenhall
                                  63396-5/ $14.95 US

THE NEW COMPREHENSIVE AMERICAN RHYMING DICTIONARY
Sue Young   71392-6/ $14.00 US/ $19.00 Can

THE PORTABLE WORLD ATLAS
Edited by B. M. Willett and David Gaylard
                                  77329-5/ $12.00 US/ $16.00 Can

THE PORTABLE WORLD FACTBOOK
Keith Lye   73051-0/ $14.00 US/ $19.00 Can